The Korean Go Association's

Learn to Play Go

Volume IV: Battle Strategies

Janice Kim 1 dan

Jeong Soo-hyun 9 dan

Drawings by Brian D'Amato

Good Move Press

Published by
Good Move Press
PO Box 6984
Denver, CO 80206
www.samarkand.net

ISBN 0-9644796-4-8

Printed in Canada

PREFACE & ACKNOWLEDGEMENTS

Edward Lasker, the well-known chess player, once said "If there are aliens, they play Go." Others have gone so far as to postulate that not only do aliens play Go, but that Go itself is a message from the aliens to us. One might wonder in that case what the aliens are trying to say.

So far in my research I've been noticing recurring patterns in Go that I speculate hold the key to the aliens' code. Many of these patterns are documented here for the first time. I've taken the liberty of naming some of them, although this was an agonizing task, as in the case of the "Alien Symbol" (the "Poodle" being a close-running second choice). Throughout the text, "I" refers to Janice Kim, who is fully responsible for errors, omissions, and mistranslations of the extraterrestrial signals I have been receiving. As a way of making the "great pronoun debate" work for us, I've adopted the convention that Black is male and White is female.

Volume IV, the continuation of the **Learn to Play Go** series, assumes knowledge of basic ideas and terms covered in the first three volumes, including dual life, eyes and eye shapes, basic capturing techniques, *haengma* or the six basic relationships between stones, basic opening theory, and counting and scoring the game. Knowledge of Go terminology is de-emphasized, although the terms *hane*, *sente*, and *atari* are used frequently and should be familiar to the reader. Key terms to know are in boldface and described within the main body of the text, or in notes below the text when a fuller description would break the flow.

This volume is designed so that any player who has read the first three volumes should have no inordinate difficulty understanding and using the information presented — with the exception of the "Extra for Experts" sections, which may require deeper study to grasp fully. However, I strongly believe that even much more experienced or higher-ranking players can benefit from studying the often-overlooked fundamentals which this book endeavors to cover.

Thanks to my family, Michael J. Simon, Brian D'Amato and the D'Amato family, David Mechner, John Lee, and Barbara London. More thanks to Liz Shura, Valerie Blum, and the extraordinary Jonathan Englander and Bruce Price.

— Janice Kim

September 1, 1997

CONTENTS

Preface and
Acknowledgements I

Part I: The Middle Game 1

① **Invasion and Reduction** 2
　1. The Difference 2
　2. Safety First 5
　3. Use Backup 7
　4. When Invading Looks Grim, Reduce 10
　5. Reducing Large Areas 16

② **Battle Strategies** 20
　1. Identifying Key Stones 22
　2. Don't Separate Living Groups 25
　3. Good Defense 26
　4. Watch Your Connections Carefully .28
　5. Don't Fear the Bogus Attack 31
　6. Fight With Purpose 33
　7. Play Aggressively Where You Are Thick 36
　8. At Times, Exchange 40

③ **How to Attack** 42
　1. Take Away the Base 45
　2. Make Profit While Attacking 48
　3. Use the Knight's Move 51
　4. Drive Towards Your Thickness 52
　5. Protect Your Own Weaknesses 54

④ **How to Take Care of Your Stones** 56
　1. Make a Base 56
　2. Make Eye Space 61
　3. Tread Lightly in Your Opponent's Area 64
　4. Take Advantage of Ko 66
　5. Give Up Hopeless Stones 68

Part II: Life and Death 71

❺ Searching for Life 72
  1. Eye Shapes 72
  2. How to Live 75
  3. The Tiger's Mouth 77
  4. The Throw-In 79
  5. Utilizing No-Parking Zones 80
  6. Dual Life 83
  7. Ko 85
  8. Playing Under the Stones to Live 88

❻ Death by Design 90
  1. How to Kill 90
  2. The Pivot 93
  3. The Alien Symbol 95
  4. The Snapback 98
  5. The Strange Property of the 2-1 Point 99
  6. Playing Under the Stones to Kill 101
  7. Dead L 102

❼ Capturing Races 106
  1. Block Outside Liberties First 106
  2. Counting Liberties 108
  3. Eye vs. No Eye 110
  3. 3-3, 4-5, 5-8, 6-12 113
  4. Big Eye vs. Small Eye 116
  5. Take Ko Last 118
  6. Don't Start If You Can't Win 120

❽ Ko Fighting 124
  1. Don't Be Afraid of Ko 124
  2. Measuring Eternity 128
  3. Picnic Ko 130
  4. Multi-Step Ko 133
  5. Double Ko 138
  6. How to Use Ko Threats 140

❾ Test Yourself 146

Index 168

PART I:

THE MIDDLE GAME

Many people feel lost in the middle game. It's true that it's hard to know if you are making mistakes in the opening, so it may seem easier. And there are more stones on the board in the middle game, so it may appear more complex. But actually there are fewer places to play in the middle game than in the opening, and you are playing with more information, so don't let the middle game throw you.

1

INVASION AND REDUCTION

1. THE DIFFERENCE

Knowing the techniques of invasion and reduction, and the difference between them, is crucial in middle-game fighting. Both techniques are used to neutralize your opponent's potential territory, but there is a big difference. In an **invasion**, you operate inside a hostile area to prevent it from becoming territory. A **reduction** works from the outside to prevent your opponent's area from getting any bigger. Invasions can be dangerous — there's a chance your stones may be killed when they are deep in your opponent's sphere of influence. Reduction is a safer way of playing. However, if an invasion succeeds, it has a greater effect than a reduction.

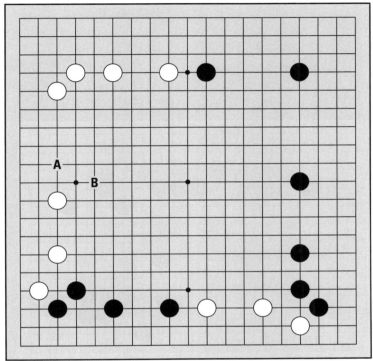

Diagram 1

Diagram 1:

Black wants to prevent White from converting the area on the left side into territory. He might consider the invasion at A or the reduction at B. Let's look at how they differ.

Diagram 2:

If Black invades at 1, White attacks at 2 and there's a big possibility that Black's stones will be trapped. This is a dangerous position, since it's difficult to live in this narrow space. However, if Black does live, White doesn't make territory in this area.

Diagram 3:

Black can reduce at 1, staying a safe distance away while preventing this area from getting bigger, but then White can make some territory with 2. Conclusion: the reduction is safer, but it has a less of an effect.

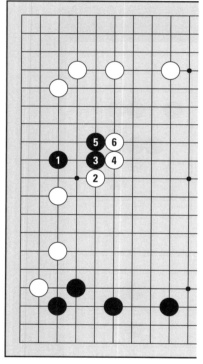

Diagram 2

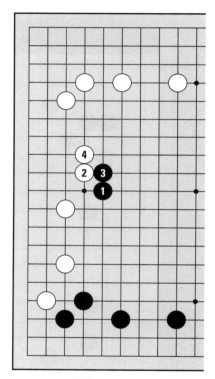

Diagram 3

Invasions and reductions have their pros and cons. If there's a big chance of getting killed, it's good to reduce. But if it doesn't seem too dangerous, an invasion is probably preferred.

2. SAFETY FIRST

When invading, the first thing you need to think about is whether or not your invading stones can live.

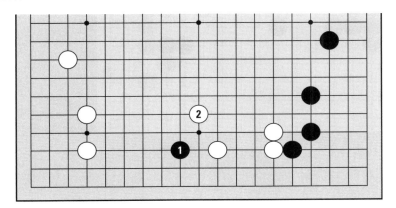

Diagram 4

Diagram 4:

Black invades at 1. If White attacks at 2, can Black live?

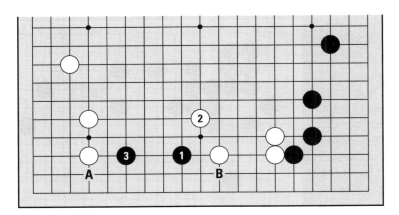

Diagram 5

Diagram 5:

Black can make a base with the two-point **extension** at 3, so this invasion is not very hazardous. (Notice Black has the option of attaching at A or B, a standard way of securing life in this kind of position.)

---

extension: generic term for a move along the side away from one of your stones, to make a base or territory.

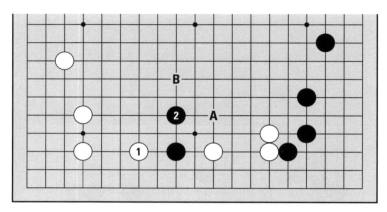

Diagram 6

Diagram 6:

What if White plays 1, taking away Black's potential base? Black can jump out at 2. Next if White A, Black can keep his head out by jumping at B, so the invasion is reasonable.

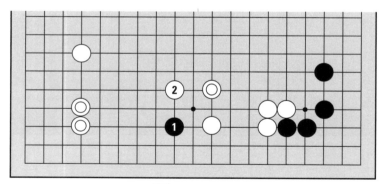

Diagram 7

Diagram 7:

What if Black invades at 1, where there is one more stone at White ◎ on the right and an **iron pillar** (the two marked stones) on the left? Then White will probably **cap** at 2. This time Black can't jump out, and he'll have difficulty making a secure base right up against White's wall of iron. In this case, the invasion is an **overplay**, or a move that tries to accomplish too much — a mistake if your opponent responds well.

---

iron pillar: two solidly-connected stones on the third and fourth lines.

cap: an opposing stone with a one-point jump relationship to a stone closer to the edge (usually on the third line).

3. USE BACKUP

It's a good idea to have backup before you invade.

Diagram 8:

The invasion at 1 is a sharp move. Because of Black ▲, White can't catch the invader.

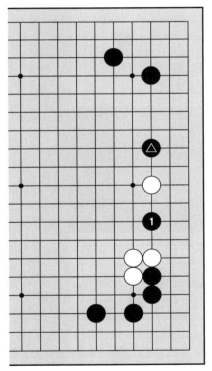

Diagram 8

Diagram 9:

White has no choice but to play at 2 and let Black connect in the sequence to 7. In this invasion, not only did Black destroy White's area, but he gained some territory as well.

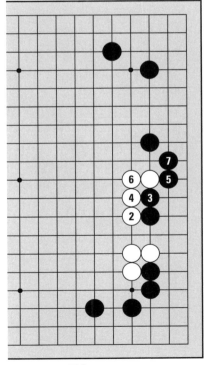

Diagram 9

Diagram 10:

If Black doesn't have backup, White can engulf the invader with the diagonal at 2. When Black pushes up at 3, White blocks at 4. If Black cuts at 5, White cuts at 6, and Black can't escape.

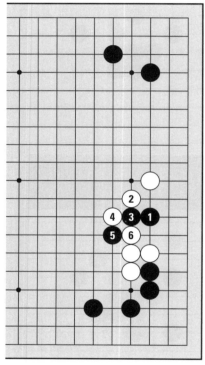

Diagram 10

Diagram 11:

White's all-or-nothing moves in the previous diagram are overplays when there's a backup stone at Black ▲. One way for Black to escape is the clever move at 5 — now Black can connect underneath at A or B.

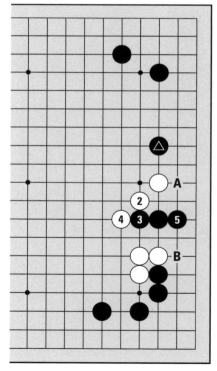

Diagram 11

Diagram 12:

The backup stone at Black ▲ makes for an easy invasion at 1.

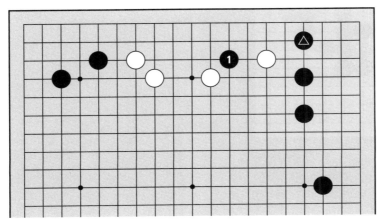

Diagram 12

Diagram 13:

Again, because of Black ▲, White has no choice but to let Black connect with 3 and 5. Most successful invasions use backup.

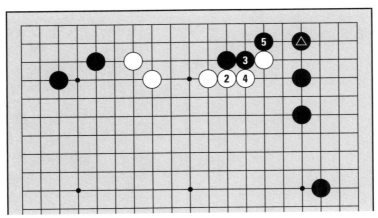

Diagram 13

4.   *WHEN INVADING LOOKS GRIM, REDUCE*

When you feel it's dangerous to invade, reducing is a better choice.

Diagram 14:

What should White do about Black's **framework**, or large potential territory?

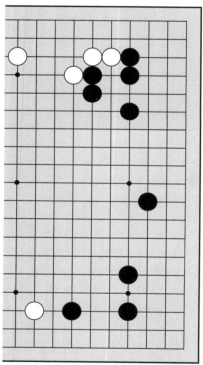

Diagram 14

Diagram 15:

If White neglects this area, Black can enlarge it with a move at 1 or A. It's difficult for White to break into this area now, but she can't allow Black to make territory of this size. White needs to do something before Black plays 1.

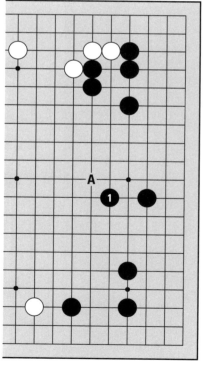

Diagram 15

Diagram 16:

What if White invades at 1 in this position? The diagonal at 2 is a good surrounding move. If White pushes out at 3, when Black plays the **hane** on top at 4, White has trouble getting out. She needs to make two eyes inside, but that looks difficult. And even if White succeeds, it will probably give Black influence that would dominate the rest of the board.

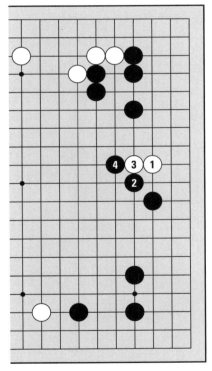

Diagram 16

Diagram 17:

What about an invasion at 1 on this side? Again, Black can seal White in with 2 and 4. Making two eyes inside is not easy. This is probably a good area to think about a reduction.

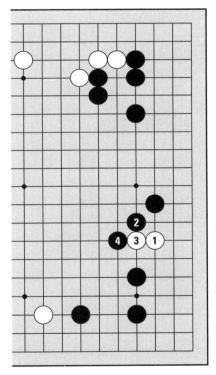

Diagram 17

Black 1 is called **turning:**

Black 1 here is a **hane,** a "quick turn" leaving a cut at A:

The cap and the **shoulder hit** are the moves used most frequently for reduction.

Diagram 18:

White caps at 1. Although Black will still make territory, this move prevents Black's area from getting bigger. White 1 is probably not going to get caught since it is out in the center.

Diagram 19:

If Black plays at 2, White can attach at 3. If Black responds at 4, White can jump at 5, further reducing Black's area and strengthening White's stones. (With 4, if Black plays the hane at A, White can just extend at B, waiting for a chance to use these stones as backup to exploit weaknesses in Black's position later.)

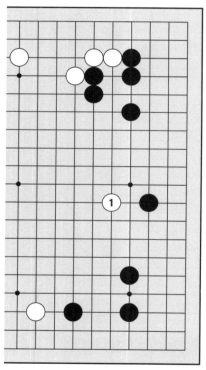

Diagram 18

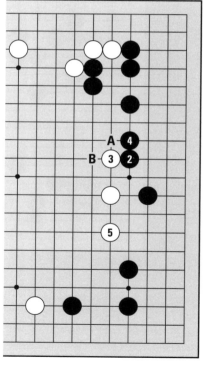

Diagram 19

---

shoulder hit: a play one line higher (usually the fourth line) with a diagonal relationship to an opposing stone.

Diagram 20:

What should Black do about White's area on the upper side?

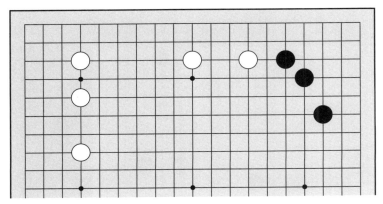

Diagram 20

Diagram 21:

An invasion at 1 here is not good. Black only has room to make a narrow extension. White can attack severely at 2 and 4.

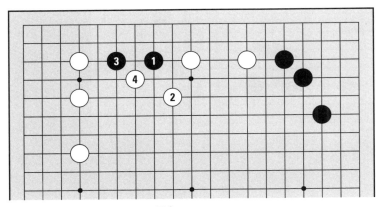

Diagram 21

Diagram 22:

In this case, a shoulder hit at Black 1 is appropriate. When a stone is on the third line, pressing it down with a cap or a shoulder hit is often a good idea.

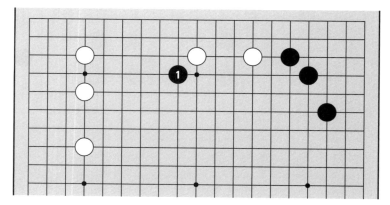

Diagram 22

Diagram 23:

If White pushes at 2, Black extends at 3. If White continues, Black keeps extending. Up to Black 11, White takes territory, and Black gets **thickness** — that is, a strong, influential group of stones. This result is good for Black, because his thickness is actually worth more than White's territory.

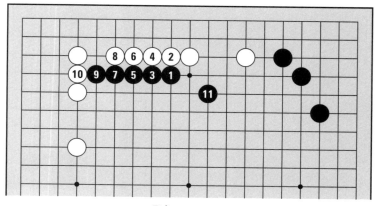

Diagram 23

Diagram 24:

Pushing once at 2 and then turning at 4 is a standard way of dealing with the shoulder hit. If Black 5, White prevents Black from making the **tiger's mouth** with 6, and Black makes a **knight's move connection** at 7. Black hasn't made thickness, but he has prevented White's area from expanding. (You may have seen in Volume I that the knight's move connection has the most scope for getting out into the center. In this case, Black 7 isn't really a connection — White can cut with White A, Black B, White C — but Black can afford to give up a small part of his group in exchange for thickness if he does get cut, so Black's not worried.)

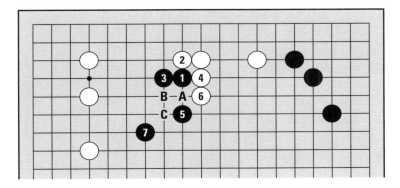

Diagram 24

Middle Game Tip: When the opponent's area is sketched out with a stone on the third line, it's often better to reduce. That's because these areas usually aren't big enough to make an invasion worthwhile, and invading stones may have trouble living with the prime base-making real estate already taken. On the other hand, if the stone is on the fourth line, you might want to consider an invasion, because the potential territory is uncomfortably large and it's a bit easier for invaders to live underneath stones on the fourth line.

In a related vein, the third line is sometimes called the **territory line,** because if you play there, it's probable your opponent will reduce and you'll end up with territory. The fourth line is called the **power line,** because if you play there, your opponent will probably invade, and you'll gain influence by attacking.

Three stones of the same color in a "V" shape is the **tiger's mouth:**

Black 1, protecting against a cut at A — with a knight's move relationship to each of the marked stones that may be cut — is the **knight's move connection:**

5. *REDUCING LARGE AREAS*

Diagram 25:

Both Black and White have built large frameworks. These areas are so big and impos-ing, it's hard to know what to do. It's White's turn — where's a good place to play?

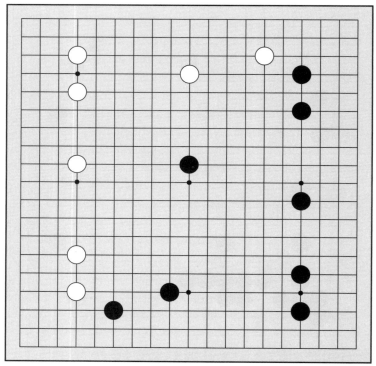

Diagram 25

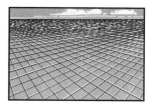

Diagram 26:

A deep invasion at White 1 is not good. You can get into trouble by invading and destroying only one part of a large framework. Capping at 2 makes center influence for Black. White can make a base and live inside, but Black can seal White in at 4. Black's still got a huge area, and now it's even harder to deal with. What White needs in this case is a move that reduces the most potential territory.

Diagram 27:

It's better to reduce from a **high** (that is, further from the edge) position at White 1. If Black 2, White can jump at 3. If Black continues to make territory with 4, White can jump out lightly at 5. This reduction successfully prevents a big part of Black's area from turning into territory.

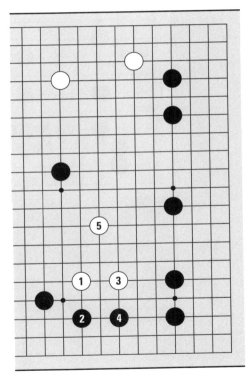

Diagram 27

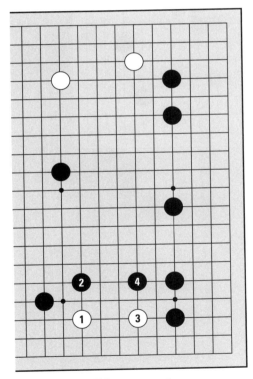

Diagram 26

Diagram 28:

Here, Black has four corners and White has influence. Black wants to prevent White from turning all her area into territory. Invading either side will make the other side stronger. How should Black approach this situation? A move that reduces all of White's area would be ideal.

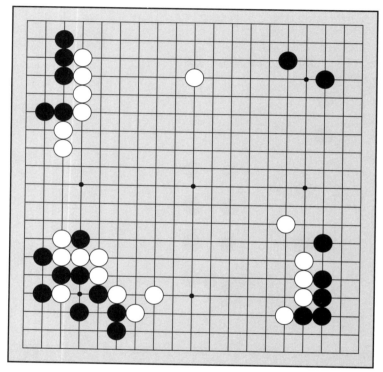

Diagram 28

Diagram 29:

Black 1, right on the center star point, is good here. (Neat translation moment: the center star point is called *tengen* in Japanese, meaning roughly "Axis of Heaven".) If White attacks at 2, Black escapes at 3. If White chases at 4, Black can even jump in the other direction at 5. Since the center is wide open, Black will probably not die. A white play at A is not that big, because Black can still jump in the area on the upper left at B.

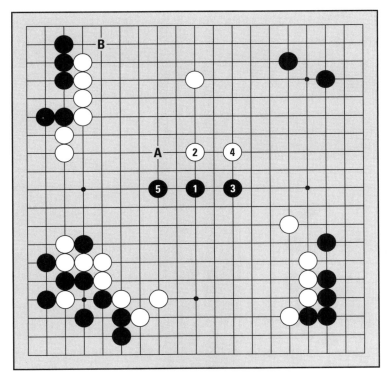

Diagram 29

When your opponent has a really large framework, keep your eye on the whole board and aim for maximum reduction.

2

BATTLE STRATEGIES

In this chapter, we'll be focusing on battles between armies on the march, as opposed to those typically arising from invasions.

Diagram 1:

When Black plays the **pincer** at 1, White jumps out at 2 and makes a counterpincer at 4. When Black jumps out at 5, White pushes at 6 and 8 and then turns her wheel sharply at 10, cutting in front of Black's stones. Black swerves to the side at 11. Both the white group on the right and Black's three-stone group are not yet alive and are on the run. This kind of fight is referred to as a running battle.

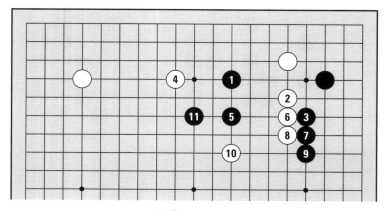

Diagram 1

pincer: move on the third or fourth line, taking away the potential base of a stone usually one, two, or three points away.

Diagram 2:

There are also contact battles, as in this position. As you might imagine, in contact battles stones are played next to each other on each other's **liberties** (the lines that emerge from a stone).

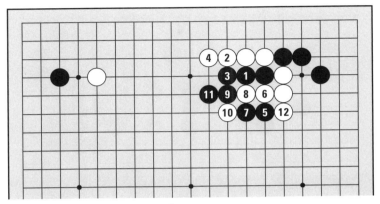

Diagram 2

In each type of battle, there are certain fundamental combat techniques you can learn to make the fight go your way.

1. IDENTIFYING KEY STONES

Some stones are currently performing a function, and others have already served their purpose. The former are called **key stones** and the latter are **expendables**. In battle, it's crucial to distinguish between the two and save the key stones.

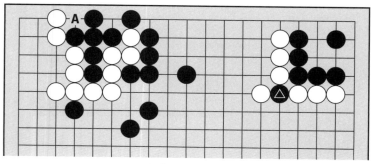

Diagram 3

Diagram 3:

On the left, if White plays at A, six black stones can be **pinned** — that is, Black can't connect all the weak points, so White can capture. On the right, Black ⚫ is in atari. Which side should Black save?

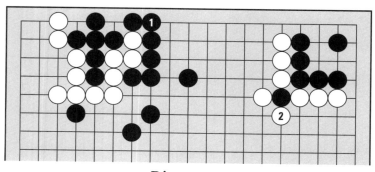

Diagram 4

Diagram 4:

If Black connects at 1 and saves the six stones, then White makes a **death star** at 2, capturing a key stone. This is an error in judgement by Black. Connecting at 1 saves six stones, but has no effect on White's group.

The **death star** (*ponnuki* in Japanese and *bbangdaerim* in Korean) is the immensely powerful four-stone diamond shape that results from the capture of a key stone. (Note that a great deal of its power stems from the fact that you have captured a stone with the minimal number of moves — just going around the board making this shape, or spending five or six moves to capture a stone, is not the same.) One experiment is to play a game where you start with a death star right smack in the center of the board. Your opponent gets all four corner star points, which should be worth at least thirty points. Find out for yourself if the Go proverb "the death star is worth thirty points" is true or not.

Diagram 5:

Black should extend at 1. Black ▲ is only one stone, but it's a key stone, keeping White split into two groups. Both groups fall under attack when Black saves the cutting stone, so it is very valuable.

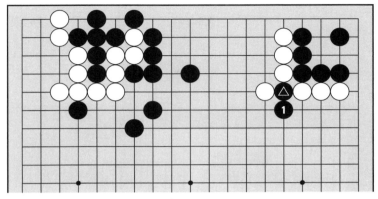

Diagram 5

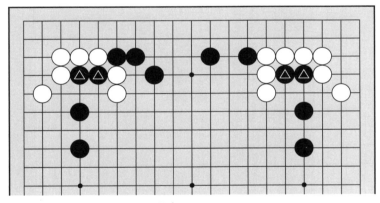

Diagram 6

Diagram 6:

Let's look at another example. White can catch the two marked black stones on the left or the two on the right. Black can only rescue one side. Which side should Black save?

Diagram 7:

Saving the stones on the left at 1 is correct. These two stones are serving an important function, namely, cutting off the marked stones from White's corner group. If Black saves the cutting stones, White will have a hard time looking after her two isolated stones floating in the center.

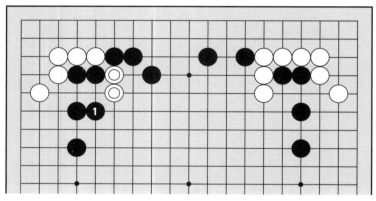

Diagram 7

Diagram 8:

Saving the stones on the right with 1 is misguided. When White catches the two key black stones at 2, all White's stones on the left are now connected. Black 1 doesn't have any effect on White's group on the right, which is already connected by the marked stone.

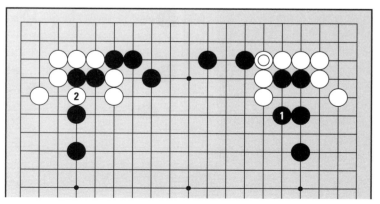

Diagram 8

2. DON'T SEPARATE LIVING GROUPS

To maintain an attack on a weak group, you have to keep it from connecting with a strong one. But separating two living groups is a little like trying to take over Newcastle by denying it coal.

Diagram 9:

Here, Black can cut White in two.

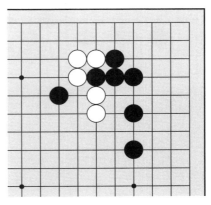

Diagram 9

Diagram 10:

Black 1 is a powerful move. Next, Black can seal in three stones at A or two stones at B. This type of cut, which makes your opponent struggle to take care of two weak forces, is very worthwhile.

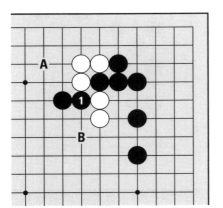

Diagram 10

Diagram 11:

This case is different. Even after Black cuts at 1, both White groups have a base, so White doesn't have anything to worry about. On the contrary, Black can be severely counterattacked with White 2.

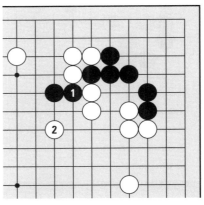

Diagram 11

3. GOOD DEFENSE

In running battles, the strongest offense is a good defense. Put another way: you can't punch very hard when you're standing on only one foot.

Diagram 12:

The battle is on in the upper right — Black jumps at 1, chasing White's two stones, White jumps at 2, and Black pushes out at 3. But then Black isn't happy when White plays the hane at 4. The Black 1–White 2 exchange actually weakened Black's group. You don't want to put your own stones in jeopardy when attacking.

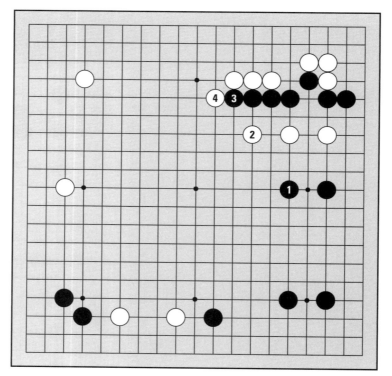

Diagram 12

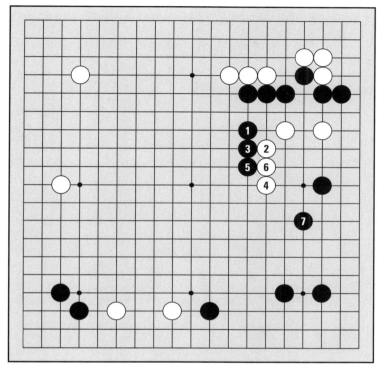

Diagram 13

Diagram 13:

In this case, it's better to jump at 1 here, putting pressure on White's stones while giving the black group some scope in the center. If White comes out at 2, Black pushes at 3 and 5, forcing White along while further strengthening Black's stones. Finally Black secures the right side with 7, and White is still saddled with a weak group. By looking out for your own stones like this you can create a favorable attacking position.

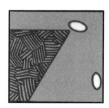

4. WATCH YOUR CONNECTIONS CAREFULLY

In a running battle, you can blow the whole game by playing moves that give your opponent a chance to cut.

Diagram 14:

In this complicated battle, the two large marked groups have run out into the center.

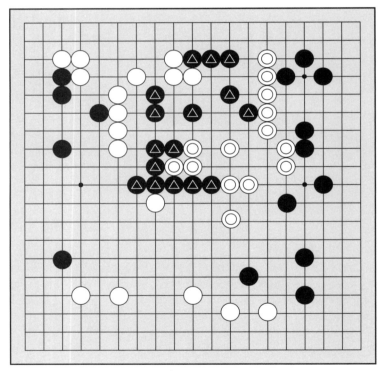

Diagram 14

Diagram 15:

Black pushes at 1 and 3 and jumps to the side with 5. But Black isn't being careful enough about his connections — he's helped create a weak point in his own group.

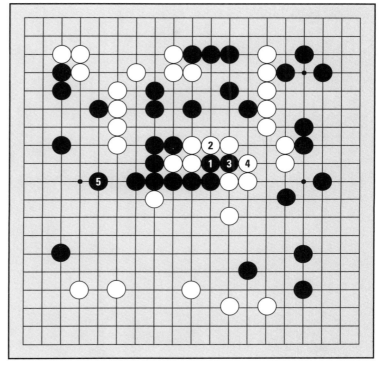

Diagram 15

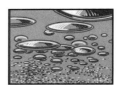

Diagram 16:

In the sequence to 7, White is able to cut the black group in two. Black has no way of connecting, since A and B **reflect** — that is, if Black plays A, White can cut at B, and if Black B, White cuts with A. Black has sustained so much damage he can't fight on any longer.

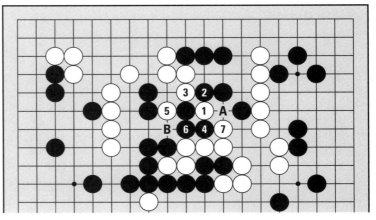

Diagram 16

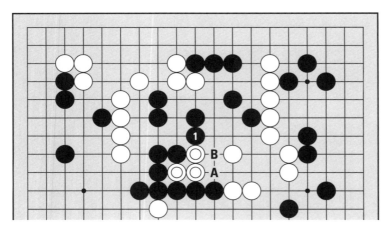

Diagram 17

Diagram 17:

Going back to the original position, we can see where the disaster started. Black exchanged Black A for White B. Once White got a stone at B, the cut was possible. Black should have played at 1 instead, securing his connection while threatening to catch the three marked stones.

A moment's carelessness about connections can cost you the game. Try to avoid unnecessary pushing and shoving, even if it forces your opponent to respond.

Two points are said to **reflect** (*miai* in Japanese and *matbogi* in Korean) when if one side plays one, the other side plays the other.

5. DON'T FEAR THE BOGUS ATTACK

Wisdom from the East: Unless you have no choice, don't try to live in a very small area. In Go, this means don't get scared in the middle of a battle and hunker down when the board is wide open. If you can, get out into the center and fight.

Diagram 18:

In six- to nine-stone handicap games, after approaching at 1 and 3, White often caps at 5, threatening the black side star point stone. The weak mentality is to get scared and struggle to live inside, like raising the drawbridge and rationing the water when you see a lone knight on the horizon.

Diagram 19:

In the moves to 12, Black is busy making a base. This negative way of playing gives White thickness on the outside and the opportunity to start new operations at 13.

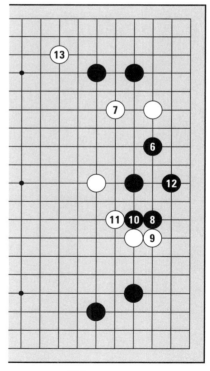

Diagram 19

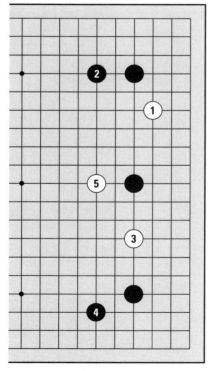

Diagram 18

Diagram 20:

After the cap, Black should come out at 2, keeping White's stones separated. If White pushes at 3 and 5, Black can counterattack with 4 and 6. Because he has a lot of stones around, this fight is good for Black.

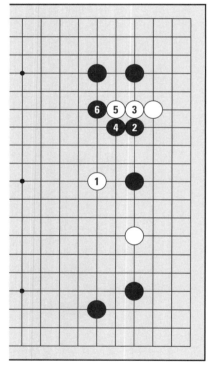

Diagram 20

Diagram 21:

Black could also come out on the other side at 2. If White jumps at 3, Black pushes into the center with 4.

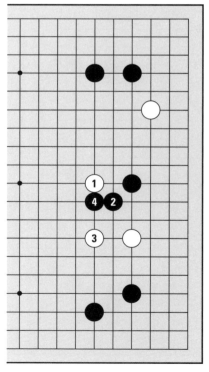

Diagram 21

6. *FIGHT WITH PURPOSE*

Don't chase groups without a specific goal in mind.

Diagram 22:

Black attacks the two white stones by capping at 1. White plays 2 and 4 to stabilize them. What should Black do now?

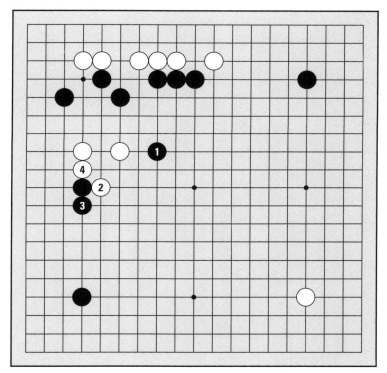

Diagram 22

Diagram 23:

What if Black attacks at 5? White pushes at 6 and 8, then jumps at 10. If Black tries to block White's path to the center at 11 and 13, White pushes at 14, Black saves one stone at 15, and White leaks out at 16. In this fight Black may feel that he is accomplishing something. In fact, he is — he's weakening his own group in the upper left.

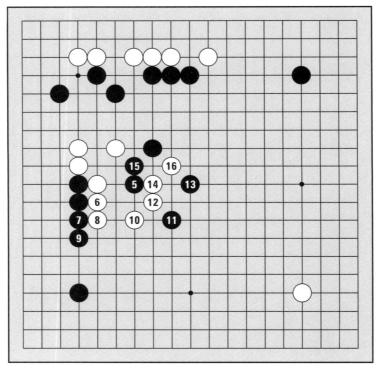

Diagram 23

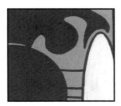

Diagram 24:

In this case, Black should push at 5 and attack with the knight's move at 7. When White jumps out, Black can secure a large area in the lower left at 9.

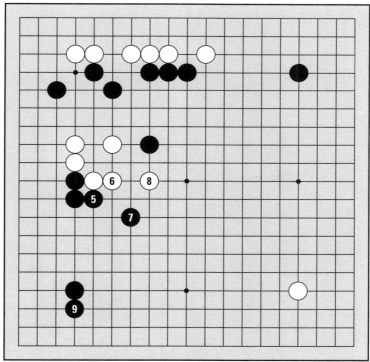

Diagram 24

7. PLAY AGGRESSIVELY WHERE YOU ARE THICK

In places where you are weak, it's wise to avoid fights and try to settle things peacefully. When you have thickness, be aggressive.

Diagram 25:

White tries to surround Black in the corner at 1. Black has a lot of stones around here — he's very thick on the left and has the marked stone on the right helping out as well. In this case, Black should play strong, aggressive moves.

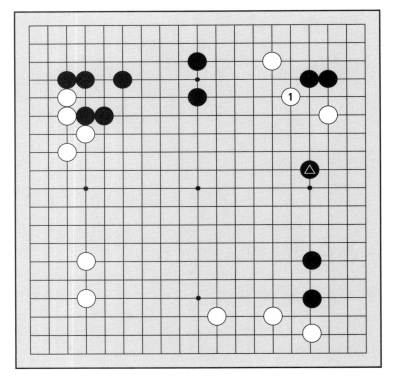

Diagram 25

Diagram 26:

Pushing and cutting with 2 and 4 is a strong way of playing. When White extends at 5, Black extends at 6, attacking the top white group. Black is in control of this fight — White will have to struggle to settle both groups.

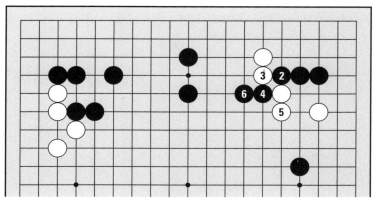

Diagram 26

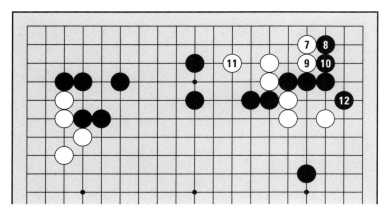

Diagram 27

Diagram 27:

White 7 and 9 are **sente** — that is, Black will have to answer these moves. Next White probably plays a move around 11. But when Black calmly makes life in the corner at 12, so far, neither white group is alive.

Diagram 28:

What happens if, after White 1, Black submissively tries to live inside at 2? Since White's 3 and 5 are sente, she can settle her group nicely with the tiger's mouth at 7. The marked stones haven't been utilized effectively, and Black has lost a good chance to take control of the game by playing aggressively in his sphere of influence.

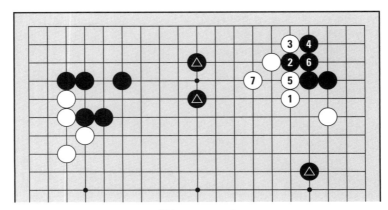

Diagram 28

Diagram 29:

What if the position looks like this, and White plays at 1? Now pushing and cutting at 2 and 4 are too aggressive. Since White has a lot of stones around here, this fight is disadvantageous for Black. After White extends at 5 —

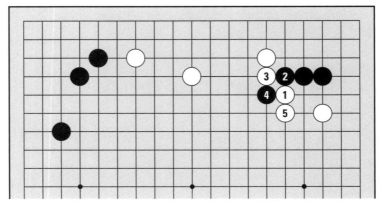

Diagram 29

Diagram 30:

If Black extends at 6, White makes the sente moves at 7 and 9, then connects the stones on top with the one-point jump at 11. Black has to live in the corner with 12, and the tables turn — now White goes on the attack at 13.

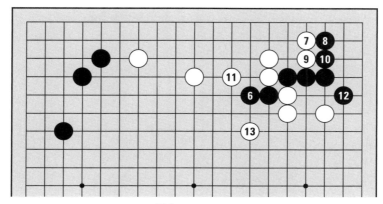

Diagram 30

Diagram 31:

In this case, it's a good idea for Black to secure life in the corner with 2, waiting for an opportunity to use this stone as backup to invade around A later.

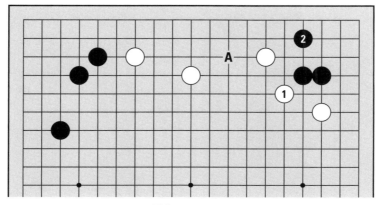

Diagram 31

Whether you live quietly and wait or cut and fight depends a great deal on the surroundings. Try to make your plans based on your resources.

8. AT TIMES, EXCHANGE

It's important to have the flexibility to make exchanges.

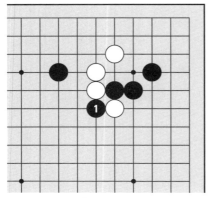

Diagram 32

Diagram 32:

Black cuts at 1, severing one white stone from the main force. How should White respond?

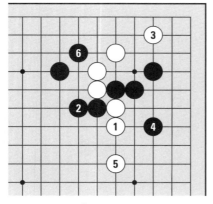

Diagram 33

Diagram 33:

If White extends at 1 to save the one stone, Black extends at 2. Now White's group on top is sealed in. If White plays at 3 to live, Black comes out at 4. If White jumps out at 5, Black can continue with 6 on a **pivot** — often the point that compromises a group's shape, leading to all sorts of nasty problems. White's hands are full trying to save both sides.

A black stone at any of the points marked A would make a tiger's mouth. A white stone at any of the points marked A would be on the **pivot.** Watch for pivots, as a play on your opponent's pivot can be enormously effective, and an opposing stone on your pivot can be a real thorn in your side.

Diagram 34:

In this case, it's better to give up one side. White plays atari at 1 and then connects with the tiger's mouth at 3. If Black catches the marked stone with 4, White engulfs a stone with 5. Making this exchange is much better than trying to save one expendable stone.

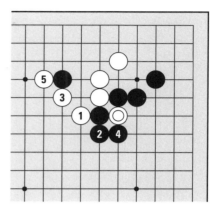

Diagram 34

3

How to Attack

To attack means to harass stones that are not alive yet, i.e., those without a base for making two eyes. Perhaps the most important basic concept in attacking is to attack with a reasonable goal in mind.

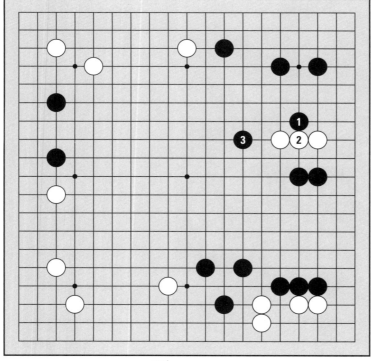

Diagram 1

Diagram 1:

On the right side, Black is on the attack. Black **peeps** at 1, making White's group **heavy**, or unwieldy and difficult to maneuver. Next Black caps at 3. Now White's group doesn't have a base or a good way of advancing into the center, so she's in danger.

Black 1 is a **peep**: a threat to cut a one-point jump.

Making a group heavy before attacking it is a good idea — it's a lot easier to catch a gang of escaping prisoners if they are all chained together. A heavy group is all stuck together in a mass, so a small part cannot be sacrificed in order to get away.

Diagram 2:

White tries to escape at 4. If Black gives chase at 5, White jumps at 6, but after Black 7, White has no way to get out into the center. If White can't make two eyes, Black can kill this group.

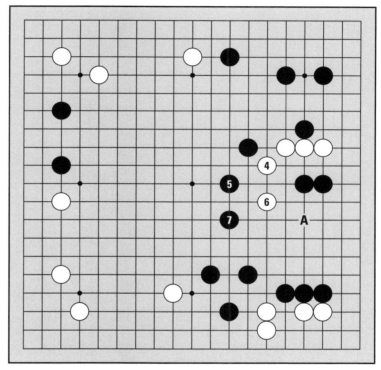

Diagram 2

But forcing White to run into Black's area to make two eyes is a very dangerous strategy. If Black fails to kill he may fall short in territory, as Black pushed White right into his area. It's unlikely that Black will kill — in fact, if White plays at A, Black may find himself struggling to live. Rather than such an all-or-nothing attack —

Diagram 3:

This attack is more realistic. After White 2, Black chases White at 3 while making territory on the right side. If White pushes at 4, even though Black can't seal White in as in *Diagram 2*, he can loosely attack White's group at 5. White 6 is about the only thing White can do, so Black builds thickness in the sequence to 9. Note that White is still not completely out of the woods.

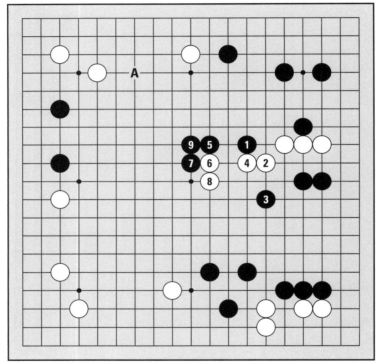

Diagram 3

In this attack, Black avoids overplaying. Even if Black doesn't kill (always a reasonable assumption, as you may remember from Volume III), Black secures territory on the right side and makes thickness in the center. Using this thickness, next Black can savage White's position in the upper left at A.

1.   TAKE AWAY THE BASE

Since you can't successfully attack a group that has a base, you need to take away the group's base before you can attack it.

Diagram 4:

How should Black attack White's lone stone on the lower side?

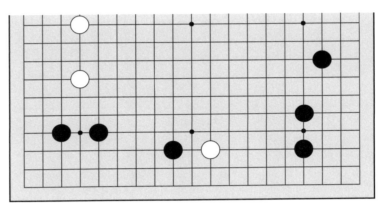

Diagram 4

Diagram 5:

Black 1 isn't an effective attack, since White can just make a base with 2. Once White has a base, it's hard to expect much from the attack.

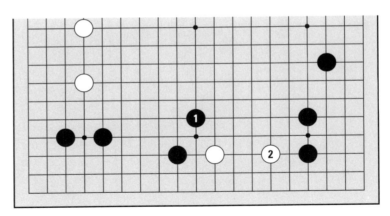

Diagram 5

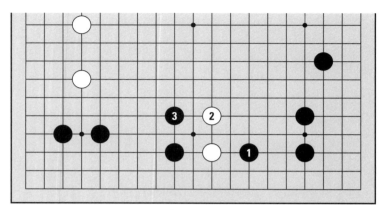

Diagram 6

Diagram 6:

Playing at Black 1 to take the base away is an auspicious beginning for an attack. As an added bonus, this move also makes a little territory. If White jumps out at 2, chasing at 3 secures Black's area on the left as well. You can profit greatly from chasing stones that don't have a base.

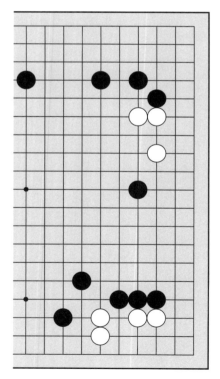

Diagram 7

Diagram 7:

How should Black attack the white group in the upper right? Try to find a move that takes away White's potential base.

Diagram 8:

If Black caps at 1, White can make a base by **sliding** at 2, settling herself while gouging out Black's territory. This is ideal for White.

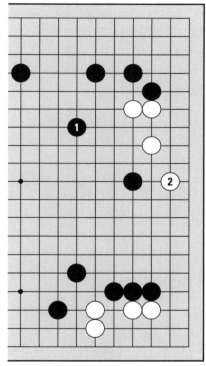

Diagram 8

Diagram 9:

The iron pillar at Black 1, taking away White's potential base, is the right way to attack. Black 1 also secures territory on the lower right side. If White jumps out at 2, Black can attack while surrounding area on the upper side with 3.

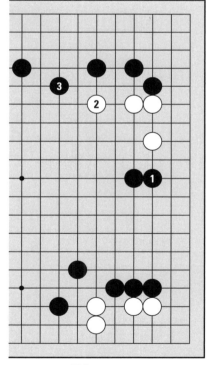

Diagram 9

Black 1 is a **slide:** a base-making play (usually on the second line) one point under an opposing stone.

2. MAKE PROFIT WHILE ATTACKING

It seems like the idea of attacking is to kill, but this is misguided. Trying to kill groups rarely succeeds unless your opponent makes big errors (a dangerous assumption) and often puts your own groups or territory at risk. You should attack in a way that makes sufficient profit to make attacking worthwhile, even if you kill nothing.

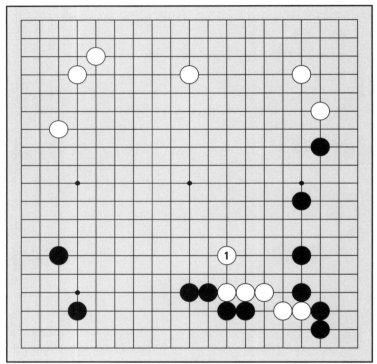

Diagram 10

Diagram 10:

The group in the lower right doesn't have a base, so White jumps out at 1.

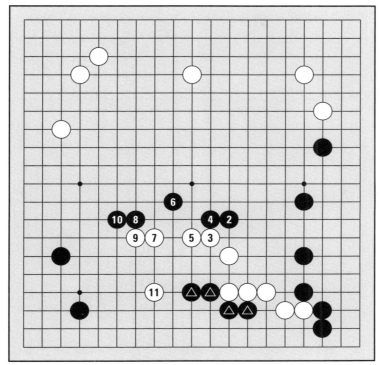

Diagram 11

Diagram 11:

It seems like a severe attack to cap at 2 and chase White's group with 4 and 6. Black can prevent White from escaping into the center at 8, but Black's own stones come under attack when White is forced to try to live inside starting with White 11. If White lives (a good assumption, given Black's problems with the four marked stones on the lower side) Black's area is destroyed.

Diagram 12:

Black must make sure to gain sufficient profit to make the attack worthwhile. Black can simply enlarge the left side by attacking with 2, 4, and 6. Next, if White plays at A, Black can play B, creating a huge framework.

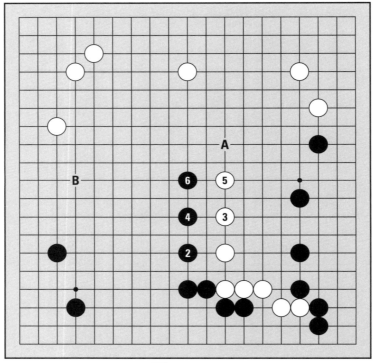

Diagram 12

3. USE THE KNIGHT'S MOVE

The speed, stability and directed force of the knight's move make it a natural for attacking.

Diagram 13:

The two black stones on the left are not alive yet. How can White attack this group and gain some profit?

Diagram 14:

The knight's move at White 1 is ideal. If Black runs at 2, then White can play another knight's move at 3. This type of knight's move attack is like a fan opening, enlarging White's area in the lower left one line with every move.

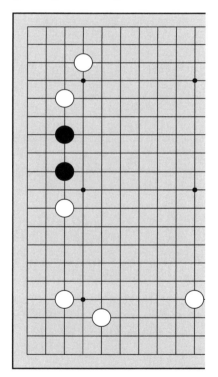

Diagram 13

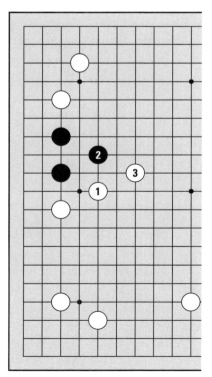

Diagram 14

4. DRIVE TOWARDS YOUR THICKNESS

Thickness is not the same thing as potential territory. You shouldn't drive your opponent towards your potential territory — those areas you've sketched out with a few stones. However, thickness — a strong, influential wall of many stones — is most effective when it is used for attack.

Diagram 15:

White jumps out at 1. How should Black attack this group?

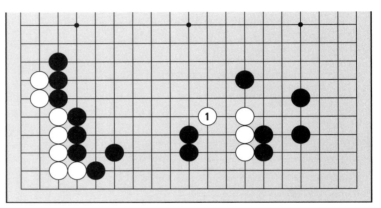

Diagram 15

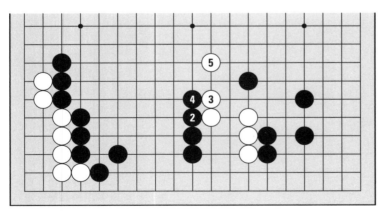

Diagram 16

Diagram 16:

If Black pushes at 2, White extends at 3. After White jumps at 5, it's hard to attack this group. Black gained a little on the left with 2 and 4, but not as much as Black could have gained by using his thickness more effectively.

Diagram 17:

In this case, forcing White to run towards Black's thickness by attacking at 2 is good. If White runs at 3, Black continues at 4. If White jumps at 5, Black can play solidly at 6. Next —

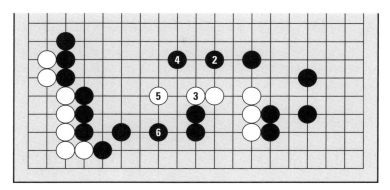

Diagram 17

Diagram 18:

If White runs with the diagonals at 7 and 9, Black seals White in with 8 and 10. White can't escape to the center, and since Black is so thick, it looks difficult for White to make two eyes inside.

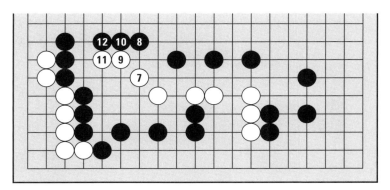

Diagram 18

Sometimes it may be difficult to tell whether you are pushing a weak group towards thickness, or towards your potential territory. One way to tell is that if you don't have to kill to benefit from the attack, you are on the right track. In *Diagram 18*, Black is completely safe, and can just sit back and watch White spend move after move struggling to make two eyes. In the meantime Black has built a tremendous wall of power in the center. This power can be used for attack, framework building, or just preventing White from making any significant territory on the rest of the board.

It may seem odd at first, but give the "drive towards your thickness" concept a try. If you just use your thickness to make territory directly, you may often fall behind in the territorial balance. That's because it's unlikely you'll make as much territory with your thickness than if you had simply sketched some territory out, and you've most likely given territory to your opponent to make the thickness in the first place. This is also a good reason why you don't want to give your opponent thickness for nothing — then anything they make is pure profit.

5. PROTECT YOUR OWN WEAKNESSES

It's a common mistake to neglect your own weaknesses when you are attacking (and as a result, for your position to fall apart if your opponent counterattacks). While attacking, remember to keep your stones secure.

Diagram 19:

This position is taken from a professional game. White's group on the right side is in danger, so White tries the weird-looking attachment at 1. Actually this move is a trap.

Diagram 20:

Suppose Black cuts off the white attachment stone in the sequence to 6. White is sealed in, so will this group die?

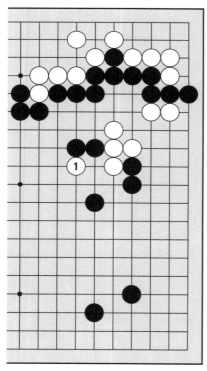

Diagram 19

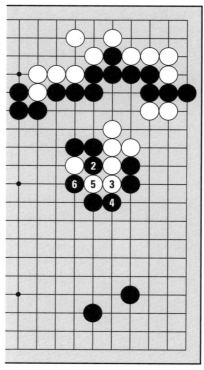

Diagram 20

Diagram 21:

In his hurry to seal White in, Black left behind a big weakness. When White counterattacks with the cut at 7, Black's moves up to 12 are necessary to save the two marked stones. Finally White plays atari at 13 and Black has no good response. A and B reflect — if Black saves the one stone in the center at B, White catches two stones at A, and if Black saves the two stones at A, White makes a death star at B. Black's failure was the result of attacking without regard to his own safety.

Diagram 22:

A more reasonable plan is to protect the cutting point at Black 2 when White attaches. When White connects with a **bamboo joint** at 3 and 5, now Black can safely attack the whole group at 6.

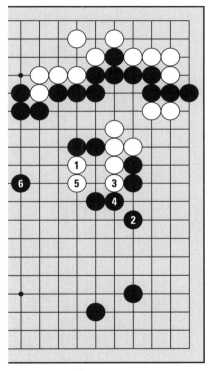

Diagram 22

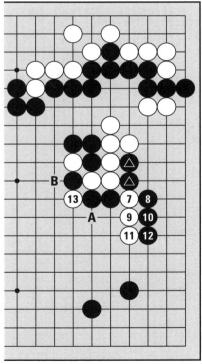

Diagram 21

Bamboo joint: four stones in this configuration have flexibility while maintaining a strong connection:

4

How to Take Care of Your Stones

1. MAKE A BASE

Often the best way to secure stones under attack is to make a base. If you have two eyes, you can't be chased around.

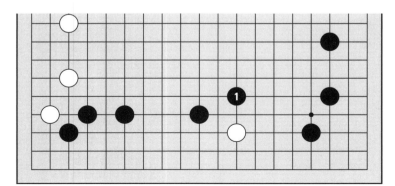

Diagram 1:

In response to White's invasion on the right side, Black capped at 1. How can White protect this stone?

Diagram 1

Diagram 2:

Making a base by sliding at 2 is best. Black 3 is about the only way to block, but then White can make life with 4 and 6 — a successful invasion for White.

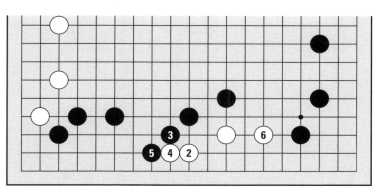

Diagram 2

Diagram 3:

Here, the two marked black stones are surrounded. They can't escape, but they can make a base inside and live.

Diagram 4:

Black 1 threatens to connect to the corner group, so White needs to block at 2. Next Black can push up at 3 and White needs to block at 4, this time to prevent Black from poking out.

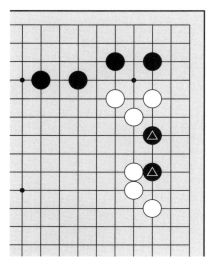

Diagram 2

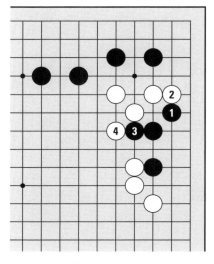

Diagram 2

Diagram 5:

Next, when Black plays at 5, White must answer at 6 to prevent Black from playing here and slicing through White's stones. Finally Black can make life with the tiger's mouth at 7. If White plays 8, Black makes two guaranteed eyes with 9.

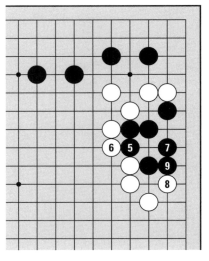

Diagram 5

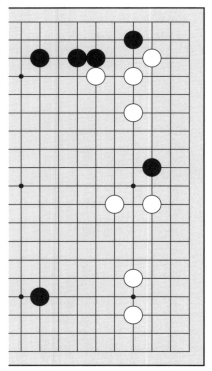

Diagram 6

Diagram 6:

In a slightly more difficult example, let's look at how to secure Black's lone stone on the right side.

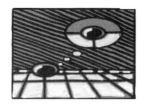

Diagram 7:

Black can escape with the one-point jump at 1, but when White peeps at 2 and takes Black's potential base away at 4, Black doesn't have even one eye. These stones are going to get chased around.

Diagram 8:

In this case, making a one-point extension at 1 is best. When White blocks at 2, Black pushes up at 3. If White extends at 4, now the one-point jump at 5 is looking better than in *Diagram 7*. Black has made one eye and can live with one more move at A.

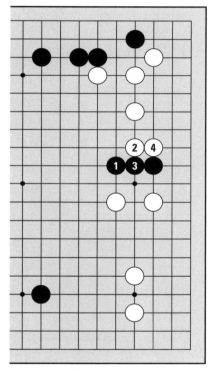

Diagram 7

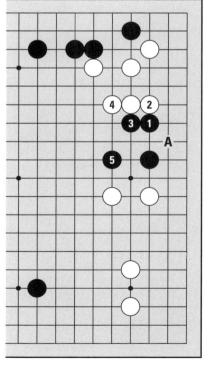

Diagram 8

Diagram 9:

If White pushes at 2, Black makes the tiger's mouth at 3. This shape has a lot of potential for making eyes. If White blocks at 4, Black makes an eye by extending at 5. White doesn't have a good attack now because Black can either escape into the center or make life on the side.

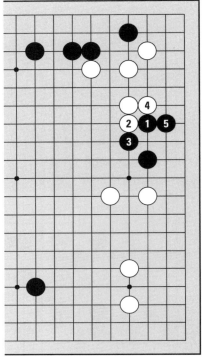

Diagram 9

There's a big difference between a group with one eye and a group with no eyes. You need two eyes to live, but to paraphrase Erasmus, in the land of the blind, the one-eyed group is truly king.

2. *MAKE EYE SPACE*

It's hard for stones in the center to live, because all four walls of their base, or **eye space,** must be constructed from scratch. That's why in the center it's especially important to make volume-enhancing moves like contact plays, and shapes with lots of eye-making potential like the tiger's mouth.

Diagram 10:

This stringy Black group doesn't have an eye, or even the potential to make an eye. Since groups like this can be easily attacked, it's best to not make them.

Diagram 11:

Here's a group that is difficult to attack because it has the potential to make eyes — for example, White can make an eye at A or surround a small area by playing at B.

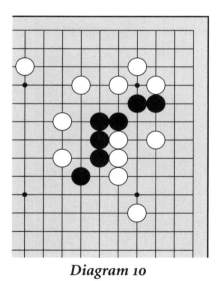

Diagram 10

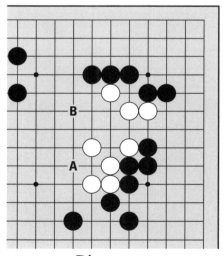

Diagram 11

Just as it can be difficult to tell "thick" and "heavy" apart, it's sometimes hard to tell if your group is like a lightning bolt blazing through a poorly-wired house, or like a helpless vegetable in a rabbit's cage. The difference: the latter (which I refer to as a String Bean Army) doesn't have eye space or eye-making potential, and is surrounded by secured enemy stones.

Diagram 12:

How can Black's group on the right side make eye space?

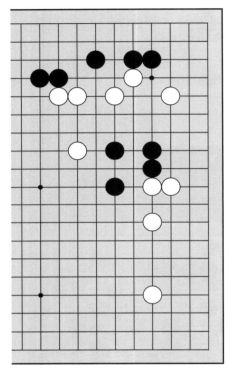

Diagram 12

Diagram 13:

Black attaches at 1. Contact plays like this attachment are a good way to make eye space. When White plays the hane at 2, Black extends at 3. When White extends at 4, Black blocks at 5, making two tiger's mouths. Now these stones can make an eye by playing at A or at B, so Black doesn't have any worries.

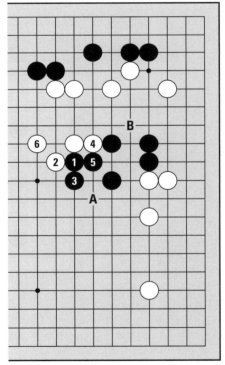

Diagram 13

Diagram 15:

White played right up against Black's side star point stone with 1 and 3. When Black extended at 4, White played a knight's move at 5, Black followed at 6, and White blew a little air into his eye-space balloon with 7. In this situation, White has already made one eye and has moves at A or B to make another, so his group is almost settled.

Diagram 14:

Let's look at an example from a game between Jeong Soo-hyun 9 dan and Suh Bong-soo 9 dan. When White played a reducing move at 1, Suh 9 dan attacked from above at 2. How can White protect his stone?

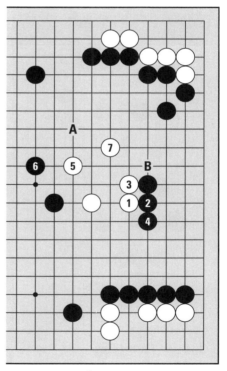

Diagram 15

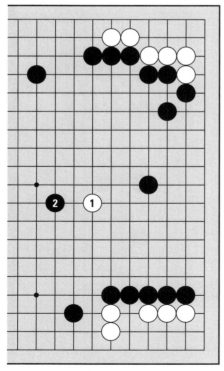

Diagram 14

3. *TREAD LIGHTLY IN YOUR OPPONENT'S AREA*

When you can't live inside your opponent's area, you have to run. In this case you should try to tread lightly.

Diagram 16:

White's three stones on the right don't have a base or any eye-making potential. How can White settle these stones?

Diagram 17:

What if White plays at 1? Black will immediately try to swallow this group whole with 2. In this situation, slow-and-steady moves like White 1 can be easily outflanked, causing serious problems. A faster and lighter move is required.

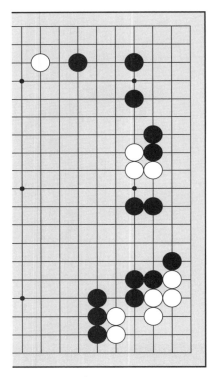

Diagram 16

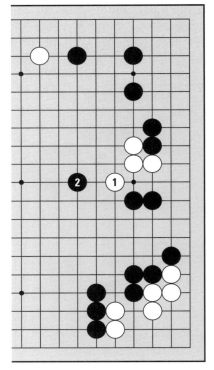

Diagram 17

You may remember from Volume II about *haengma*, or the Way of the Moving Horse. *Haengma* are the six basic relationships: from one of your stones, you can extend, play the diagonal, the one-point jump, the knight's move, the two-point jump, or the large knight's move. The rule is: the farther apart the stones are, the faster and lighter the *haengma*.

Diagram 19:

White 1 is best. In your opponent's area, it's a good idea to "float like a butterfly" with fast and light *haengma* like this two-point jump. Black can't find a good move to harass these stones now — if he caps at A, White can jump at B, and if he chases White at B, White can jump at A.

Diagram 18:

How about the one-point jump at 1? This is better than the diagonal in *Diagram 17*, but it's still too slow —Black can still attack at 2. White can jump further out and retain connectivity. Notice White A is sente (Black should answer, in this case at B) so after the A–B exchange, White will have three stones in a row. Generally from a wall of three stones you can jump at least two points without any worries that your stones can be cut.

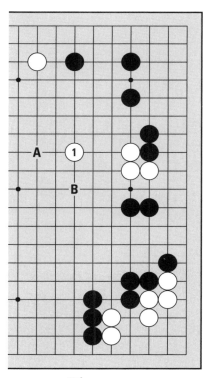

Diagram 19

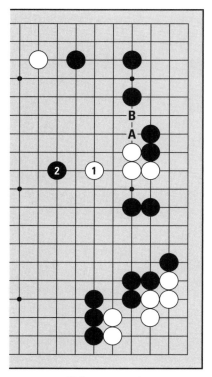

Diagram 18

4. TAKE ADVANTAGE OF KO

Ko can be your friend, especially when settling weak stones.

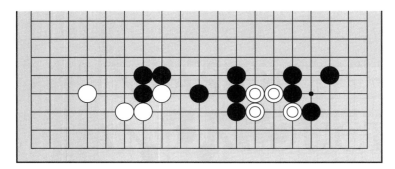

Diagram 20

Diagram 20:

In the lower right, White's four marked stones are in great danger. How can White save them?

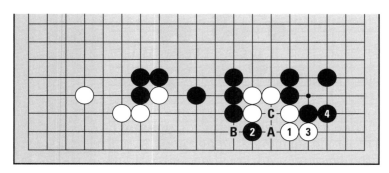

Diagram 21

Diagram 21:

Trying to make a base by extending at 1 gets this group killed when Black plays the hane at 2. If White pushes at 3 Black extends at 4. If White A, Black can connect at B, making C a **false eye** — it looks like an eye, but White's stones aren't all connected. Ordinary moves like White 1 won't take care of the problem.

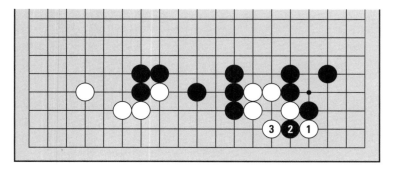

Diagram 22

Diagram 22:

The hane at White 1 is best. If Black plays atari at 2, White makes a ko at 3. If you can't secure unconditional life for your stones, you should try at least to make a ko.

Diagram 23:

If Black takes the ko at 4, White can play the hane at 5, threatening to connect to the group on the left. Black blocks at 6 and White takes the ko back at 7.

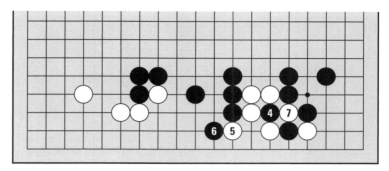

Diagram 23

Diagram 24:

Next if White ignores a ko threat and captures a stone at A, winning the ko, White is alive. Black's not thrilled with this ko, since if he loses it, he also loses a lot of corner territory. Furthermore, White has some handy ko threats at B and C.

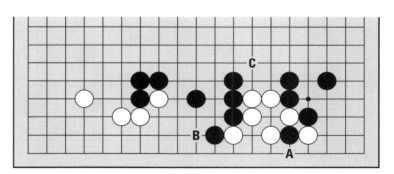

Diagram 24

Diagram 25:

When White plays the hane at 1, what happens if Black extends at 2 to avoid the ko? White can make life with the tiger's mouth at 3.

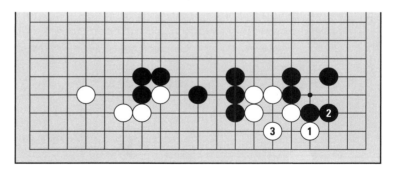

Diagram 25

Ko-making is a difficult art to master — for now, just try to look for ways to make a ko out of situations where your stones look like they've had it.

5. GIVE UP HOPELESS STONES

There are times when an attack is so powerful that you cannot save your stones. Logically, you should just give up stones which have no hope of survival or escape. Emotionally this can be difficult, but trying to save mortally wounded soldiers often results in heavier losses.

Diagram 26:

With White ◎, Black's invading force on the left side is in trouble. White's nearby thickness makes escape look very difficult. What is the best plan for Black?

Diagram 27:

Even if one suspects these stones can't escape, it's very tempting to just try to pull them out. In the sequence to 8, Black gets completely sealed in. Black has a little breathing room, but it would take a miracle for him to make two eyes.

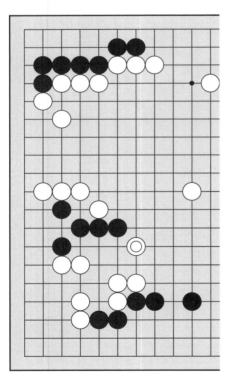

Diagram 26

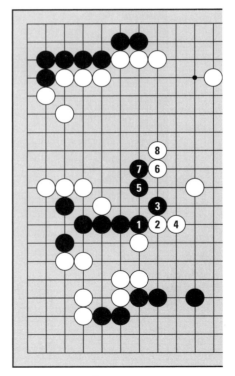

Diagram 27

Diagram 28:

In this case, it's a good idea to give up the stones on the left with Black 1. Then when White cuts them off at 2, Black pushes at 3, neutralizing White's influence in the center.

If you realize they are beyond help, it's best to give up stones that have withered on the vine and try to get something from the "sacrifice." I call this the "I planned that three months ago" attitude.

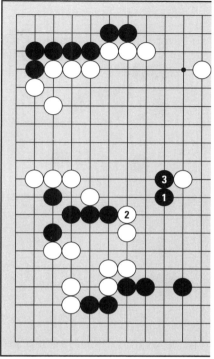

Diagram 28

PART II:

LIFE AND DEATH

Determining which groups are alive and which are dead is one of the most important components of the game. The ability to read, or to anticipate move sequences, is the key to life and death. But first, there are some basic concepts about eye shapes and techniques for making and destroying eyes to learn, so you'll know what to look for when you're reading.

5

Searching for Life

1. Eye Shapes

If a group's eye shape cannot be reduced to fewer than seven points, it's probably more accurate to say the group has territory, rather than an eye shape. Another way of looking at it is that eye shapes of seven points or more are alive — you can make two eyes, or at least dual life, in spaces this large. (Keep in mind, however, that you always need to be on the lookout if your stones are not all solidly connected — a space-reducing, potentially lethal atari may be in your future).

All eye shapes boil down to ten basic formations: straight three, bent three, straight four, three kinds of bent fours (the "L", the "T", and the "Z"), square four, radial five, flower six, and rectangular six. It may seem like a lot to remember at first, but if you are conversant with these basic formations, you are well on your way to being a master at life and death.

Diagram 1:

The black group's eye shape on the left is the **L bent four,** on the right, the **straight four,** and in the middle, the **Z bent four.** All these groups are alive just as they are, because White can't prevent Black from making two eyes even if it's her turn.

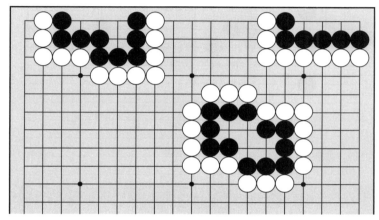

Diagram 1

Diagram 2:

In the upper left is a **bent three,** in the upper right a **straight three,** and in the middle a **T bent four.** In all these cases, Black needs to play a stone in the center of each eye shape to live. (If the marked stone is pushed out to give an extra point inside the T, the resulting shape is what I call the "Maltese five" — Black needs a stone in the center to live here too.)

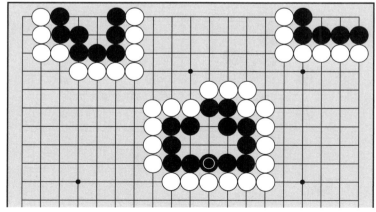

Diagram 2

Diagram 3:

With both the **radial five** on the left and the **flower six** on the right, Black needs to play at A to live. A is also the vital point for White to kill.

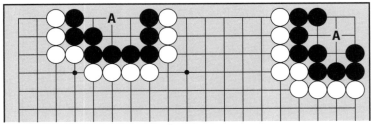

Diagram 3

Diagram 4:

The **square four** on the left is dead even if it's Black's turn to play. On the right, **rectangular six** is alive. It's better to think of these groups as "alive" or "dead", rather than thinking if you could play twice, you could live with the square four, or kill the rectangular six. It's not very useful to speculate how you or your opponent might get in two moves in a row, since that would be relying on one player's having a seizure in the middle of the game.

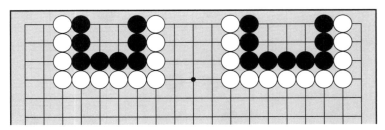

Diagram 4

The upshot: The status of three-point eye shapes is undetermined. Of the four-point eye shapes, all are alive except the T bent four (undetermined) and the square four (dead). All five-point eye shapes are alive, except the radial five and the Maltese five (both undetermined). All six-point eye shapes are alive, except the flower six (undetermined). All eye shapes with seven points or more are alive. Remember, an eye shape is eye space that is completely surrounded, by stones that are all connected.

Special note: We have been calling the vital point — the point that determines life and death of a group if it is not already alive or dead as it stands — the "center" or the "center of symmetry." There's also an interesting way of looking at it in terms of pivots. The pivot, you may recall, is an opposing stone on the unoccupied "jaw" of a just-about-to-be-formed tiger's mouth. The vital point of an eye shape is always on a pivot. For example, the vital point of the radial five in *Diagram 3* is on two pivots. I call the shape that results when there is a killing stone on this pivot the "blown-out radial."

2. HOW TO LIVE

There are two techniques for living when your group is surrounded and needs to make two eyes: enlarging the base, and playing at the vital point.

Diagram 5:

Try to save this white group.

Diagram 6:

The hane at 1 and descent to 3 enlarges the base to its maximum size. Making the rectangular six eye shape is the only sure way to live here.

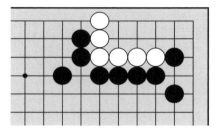

Diagram 5

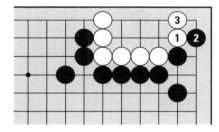

Diagram 6

Diagram 7:

The rectangular six is alive because it has two "center" points that reflect; if Black 4, White plays 5, and if Black 5, White 4. Reading further, if Black plays at A here, White plays B, and if Black plays B, White plays A.

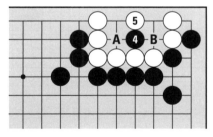

Diagram 7

Note: As you may have seen in Volume II, if all the stones in an otherwise living eye shape are not all solidly connected to each other, you need to make sure no lethal atari is coming up. For example, here when Black plays at 1 and White plays 2, after Black cuts at 3, White can't play at A to make the second eye, because that would be putting her own group in atari. The marked stone is blocking a liberty that turns the living group in *Diagram 7* into a killable group here.

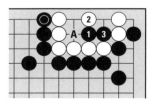

Diagram 8:

How does White live here? Since White's small living room can't be expanded much further, she needs to put a stone in a strategic spot to make this area livable.

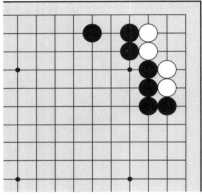

Diagram 8

Diagram 9:

If White had tried to enlarge the base with 1, Black could play the hane at 2. White can't block at A (do you see why?) and a play at 3 makes the radial five, which can be killed by playing on the pivot at 4.

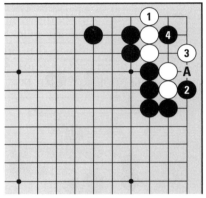

Diagram 9

Diagram 10:

In this case, White needs to play at 1 first to live.

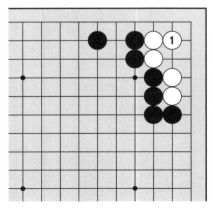

Diagram 10

Diagram 11:

What if Black attacks at 2? White blocks at 3, and if Black 4, White lives by connecting at 5.

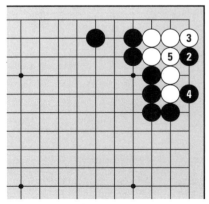

Diagram 11

3. THE TIGER'S MOUTH

The tiger's mouth has a kind of built-in eye structure, so it's often very useful in life-and-death situations.

Diagram 12:

How can Black live?

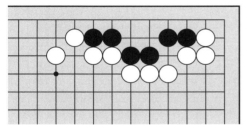

Diagram 12

Diagram 13:

If Black tries enlarging his base at 1, White can kill by playing on the pivot at 2. (Try to confirm for yourself that A and B reflect and Black is dead.)

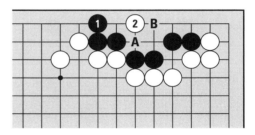

Diagram 13

Diagram 14:

Since maximizing the size of Black's base doesn't work, he should play the tiger's mouth to make two eyes. (For mental exercise, try to figure out how White can kill if Black plays the other tiger's mouth at A.)

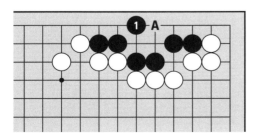

Diagram 14

Diagram 15:

If White plays the hane at 2, Black lives by playing at 3.

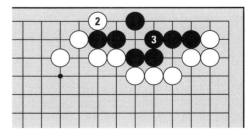

Diagram 15

Diagram 16:

This group needs to make another eye on the edge.

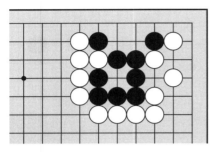

Diagram 16

Diagram 17:

If Black connects at 1, White plays atari at 2. Black's only chance then is to play at A and try to live by ko.

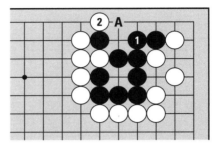

Diagram 17

Diagram 18:

Black can live here with the tiger's mouth at 1. (Notice the tiger's mouth at A also works here.) If White 2, Black connects at 3, forming the second eye.

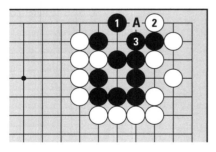

Diagram 18

Diagram 19:

If White tries to catch a stone at 1, Black can descend at 2. Because of Black ⬤, if White then plays atari at A, Black can link up on the first line at B.

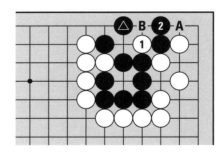

Diagram 19

Imagine Black starts a ko for life by blocking at A as in *Diagram 17*. After White takes the ko, suppose Black plays a ko threat, White answers the threat, and Black takes back the ko. Next, White can connect at B as an **internal ko threat** — that is, a threat associated with the ko itself, that must be answered or fighting the ko becomes meaningless. Black has to respond to this threat by playing C to try to make the second eye, so White can then take back the ko.

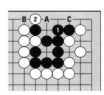

4. THE THROW-IN

The throw-in, discussed in previous volumes, is one of the most commonly used capturing techniques in life-and-death situations.

Diagram 20:

Black must use White's weaknesses here to live.

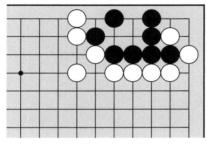

Diagram 20

Diagram 21:

If Black plays atari at 1, White simply connects at 2.

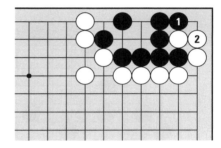

Diagram 21

Diagram 22:

With the throw-in at 1, Black can live. When White takes at 2, the atari at Black 3 pins two white stones.

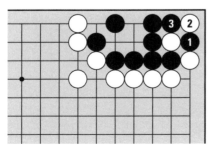

Diagram 22

Diagram 23:

In this position, how can Black live? He'll need to utilize the throw-in.

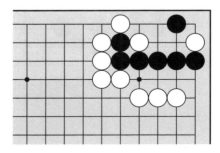

Diagram 23

Diagram 24:

If Black plays atari at 1, White connects at 2 and Black only has one eye.

Diagram 25:

The throw-in at Black 1 is the key. When White takes at 2, Black can play atari at 3, pinning two stones.

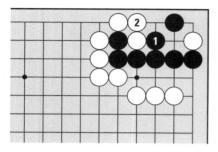

Diagram 24

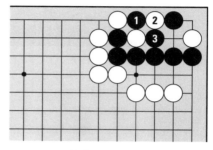

Diagram 25

5. *UTILIZING NO-PARKING ZONES*

Diagram 26:

Can the black group in the corner make two eyes?

Diagram 27:

If Black plays atari at 1, Black dies with White 2.

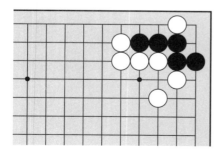

Diagram 26

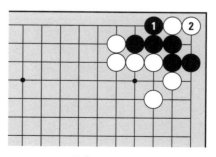

Diagram 27

Diagram 28:

Again, Black should play the throw-in. (It's a throw-in because Black 1 is actually in atari.) If White takes at 2, it looks like a ko, but —

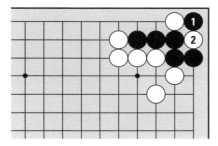

Diagram 28

Diagram 29:

When Black plays atari at 3, White can't connect, because that would be playing on a point with no liberties without capturing (one of the few prohibitions on where you can park your stones). Therefore Black is alive.

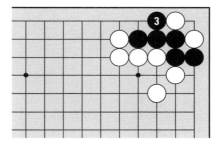

Diagram 29

Diagram 30:

If Black wants to live in the corner here, he must use the same technique of creating a New York-style no-parking zone to prevent White from taking the vital spot.

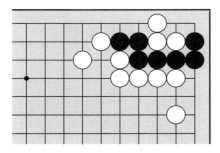

Diagram 30

Diagram 31:

If Black 1, White can kill at 2. (To take Black's stones off the board, White can block all the outside liberties, then play atari at A. If Black captures, the resulting position is the radial five eye shape with White's turn to play — White kills by playing on the pivot.)

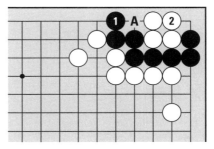

Diagram 31

Diagram 32:

Black needs to play the throw-in at 1 first. When White takes at 2 —

Diagram 33:

Black plays atari at 3. White is not allowed to make a move at A, so Black is alive.

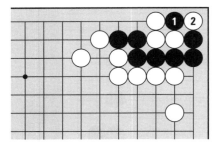

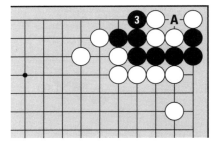

Diagram 32

Diagram 33

In an alternate rule system proposed by the late Mr. Ing Chang-ki, one may play "self-removal" — an illegal move in other rule systems — by playing on a point with no liberties without capturing. For example, White could play at A in *Diagram 33* and take her own stones off. This doesn't change the life-and-death status of the black group, though, because self-removal counts as a whole turn. After White plays A and removes her stones, Black can then live by playing at the center of the resulting radial five. What's the difference, then? When there's a situation where a no-parking zone has been utilized to live in a small space, self-removal can be used as a ko threat.

6. DUAL LIFE

The situation in which groups co-exist without two eyes is dual life (*seki* in Japanese and *beek* in Korean), discussed in previous volumes.

Diagram 34:

Black can't make two eyes. But he can make dual life.

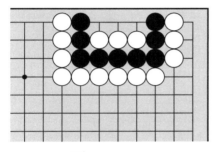

Diagram 34

Diagram 35:

Black 1 is the key.

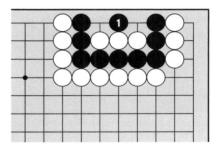

Diagram 35

Diagram 36:

If White tries to kill at 2, Black captures at 3, making the L bent four.

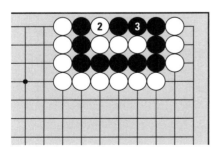

Diagram 36

Diagram 37:

This is the result after Black captures. This shape is alive, so after *Diagram 35*, the best White can do is dual life.

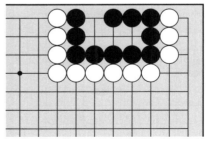

Diagram 37

Diagram 38:

It looks like Black has a big base to work with, but actually it's not easy for him to live.

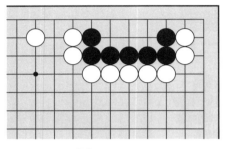

Diagram 38

Diagram 39:

If Black tries to enlarge the base at 1, White can kill by playing the hane at 2 and then the pivot at 4.

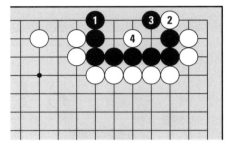

Diagram 39

Diagram 40:

Black can make dual life by making two tiger's mouth formations at 1.

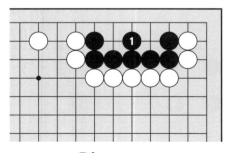

Diagram 40

Diagram 41:

If White tries to kill, the sequence to 6 makes dual life. Neither side has any territory here, but Black survives.

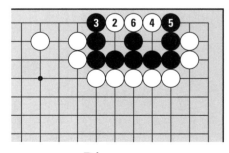

Diagram 41

7. Ko

When you're surrounded and can't make two eyes or dual life, try to make a ko.

Diagram 42:

This shape occurs frequently in real games. How should White play?

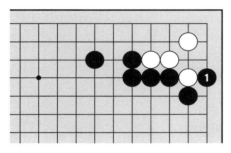

Diagram 42

Diagram 43:

Connecting at 1 gets White killed when Black plays the hane at 2.

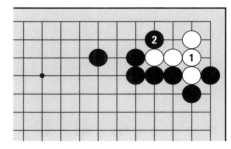

Diagram 43

Diagram 44:

The sequence of the hane at 1 and tiger's mouth at 3 doesn't work either if Black attaches at 4.

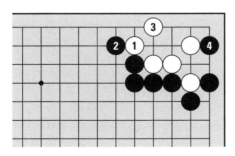

Diagram 44

Diagram 45:

Starting a ko with the atari at 1 is White's only hope.

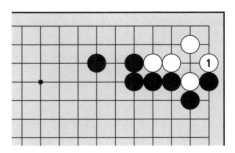

Diagram 45

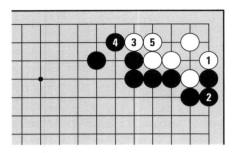

Diagram 46

Diagram 46:

If Black gives in by connecting at 2, White lives with the hane and connection at 3 and 5.

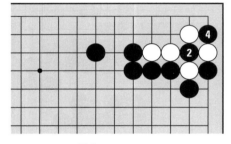

Diagram 47

Diagram 47:

If Black takes the ko with 2, White can play a ko threat elsewhere on the board with 3. If Black ignores White's threat and wins the ko by capturing at 4, White can be compensated for the loss of the corner by following up on the threat, a significant improvement from just dying for nothing as in *Diagram 43*.

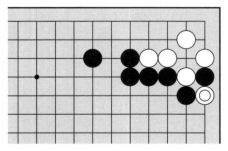

Diagram 48

Diagram 48:

If Black loses this ko, the capture at White ◎ secures life for the corner, and Black's position on the left side is compromised by the White group streaming through the hole on the edge.

Diagram 49:

The group in the corner looks nearly dead, but Black can make a ko.

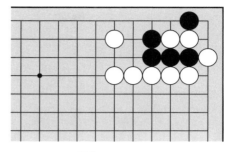

Diagram 49

Diagram 50:

If Black plays atari at 1, White simply connects at 2. It's the end of the line for Black.

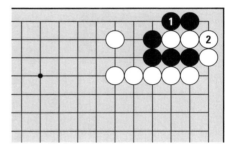

Diagram 50

Diagram 51:

Black can start a ko with the throw-in at 1. Even if White wins the ko, Black should be able to get some compensation.

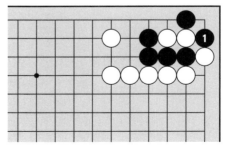

Diagram 51

8. PLAYING UNDER THE STONES TO LIVE

This is an interesting sacrifice technique involving a bit of reading.

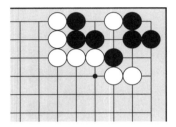

Diagram 52

Diagram 52:

It looks like Black has two eyes, but there is a small problem.

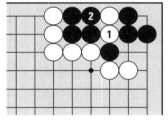

Diagram 53

Diagram 53:

If White plays the throw-in at 1 and Black takes at 2 —

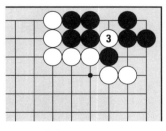

Diagram 54

Diagram 54:

White can play the throw-in at 3 again. How would you play?

Diagram 55:

Black must connect at 4 to live. (If Black captures at 5 instead, White at 4 makes Black's second potential eye false.) White 5 captures four stones, but —

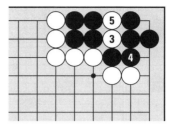

Diagram 55

Diagram 56:

Black 6, playing under the stones, captures White's two stones. With this Black is alive.

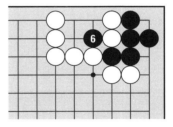

Diagram 56

6

DEATH BY DESIGN

1. HOW TO KILL

Just as there are two main techniques for living, there are also two corresponding killing techniques: reducing a group's base, and playing on a group's vital point.

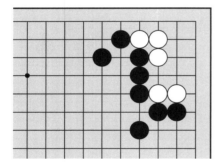

Diagram 1

Diagram 1:

If Black plays first, he can kill the corner group.

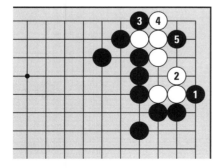

Diagram 2

Diagram 2:

The hane at 1, reducing the base, is a good example of the Go proverb "There is death in the hane". White is pretty much limited to answering at 2. Then Black plays the other hane at 3. If White blocks at 4, Black kills by playing the vital point at 5.

Diagram 3:

When Black plays the hane at 1, what if White tries playing the vital point herself at 2 instead of blocking? Black can still kill by playing at 3, then pushing in at 5 and preventing the second eye with 7. If White takes at A, this only makes a false eye when Black plays the throw-in at 1.

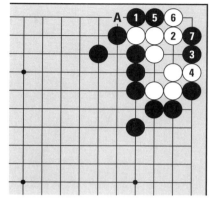

Diagram 3

Diagram 4:

If Black plays at 1 to take the vital point first, White can play at 2. Then if Black pushes in at 3, White can give up two stones and live with the main group by playing at 4 (if Black A, White B, and if Black B, White A, so White can make two eyes).

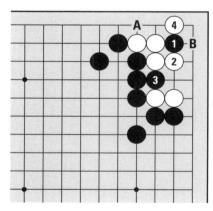

Diagram 4

Diagram 5:

Try to kill this white group.

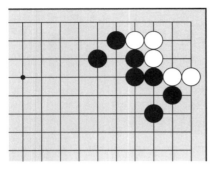

Diagram 5

Diagram 6:

In this case, if Black plays the hane at 1 to reduce the base, White lives with 2.

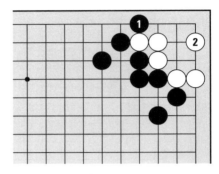

Diagram 6

Diagram 7:

Here, Black needs to take the vital point at 1 first. White doesn't have any way to live.

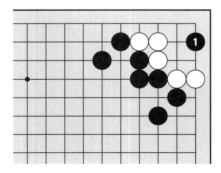

Diagram 7

Diagram 8:

If White 2, Black can kill by just blocking at 3 — White's dead because Black has a clever way of capturing the two marked stones with a throw-in at A, and a White connection at A doesn't give her two eyes. (In fact, White 4 at A would be a tragic waste, since her group would still be dead, without Black having to do anything.)

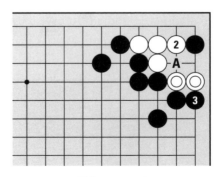

Diagram 8

2. THE PIVOT

The pivot, an opposing stone on one of the "jaws" of a just-about-to-be-formed tiger's mouth, is often key in the prevention of two eyes.

Diagram 9:

It may look difficult to kill the corner group, but if Black plays on the pivot, White is helpless.

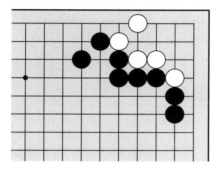

Diagram 9

Diagram 10:

If Black just captures a stone at 1, White lives with 2 and 4.

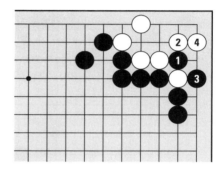

Diagram 10

Diagram 11:

The killing play is the pivot at Black 1. When White connects at 2, Black extends at 3 to destroy a potential eye. Next —

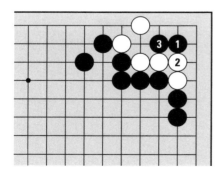

Diagram 11

Diagram 12:

If White connects at 4, Black plays the hane at 5 to reduce the base. If White plays the hane at 6, Black 7 kills (try to confirm this for yourself).

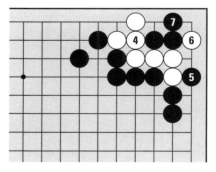

Diagram 12

Diagram 13:

Try to kill White by playing on a pivot.

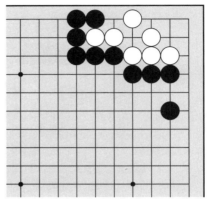

Diagram 13

Diagram 14:

If Black just plays atari at 1, White lives at 2. If Black takes White's two stones, White takes one stone back and lives. (This isn't a ko — when White takes one stone back, her capturing stone is not then in atari.)

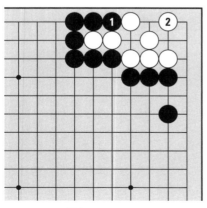

Diagram 14

Diagram 15:

Here, Black 1 is on the pivot. With this move, White is dead. Since A and B reflect (if White plays A, then Black plays B, and if White B, Black A), White can't make two eyes.

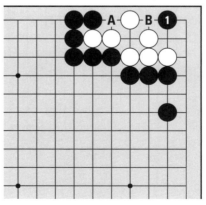

Diagram 15

3. *The Alien Symbol*

Some aliens contacted me, and told me about this.

Diagram 16:

These black and white stones form the basic Alien Symbol. The marked stone occupies the crucial point preventing the formation of the bamboo joint. The other two white stones complete the key that unlocks a door to a secret armory of magical weapons.

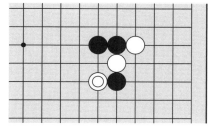

Diagram 16

Diagram 17:

Here's an example. White is cut and doesn't have a base on either side. It looks pretty grim, but if White knows the Alien Symbol, she can connect her groups by capturing Black's two marked stones.

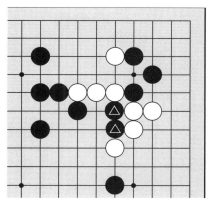

Diagram 17

Diagram 18:

The four marked stones have started to form the Alien Symbol. There remain two unplayed points at A and B, so White should have a look at these moves. If White plays at A—

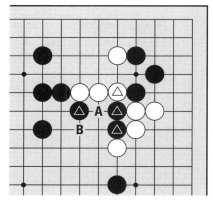

Diagram 18

Diagram 19:

Black is in atari, so he comes out at 2. Next White can play double atari at 3, and Black can't save both sides. But when you play double atari, your opponent gets to choose which side to save. In this case, Black will save the two key stones separating White's groups.

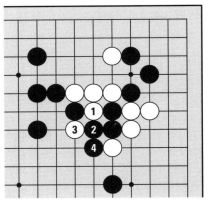

Diagram 19

Diagram 20:

White A didn't work to capture the two black stones, so what about the strange-looking move at B, preventing the bamboo joint?

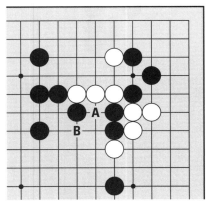

Diagram 20

Diagram 21:

Black sees that White will catch the two stones for certain if next White plays at 2, so he could try playing there first. But then White can cut at 3 and all four of Black's stones are trapped.

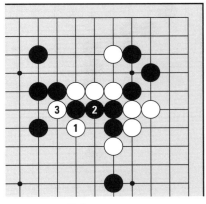

Diagram 21

Diagram 22:

What if Black tries to escape by playing at 2? White blocks at 3, pinning three Black stones.

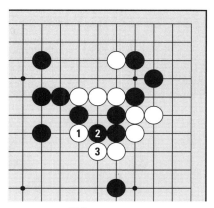

Diagram 22

Diagram 23:

Last ditch effort — Black plays the hane at 2. Here White just cuts at 3 and pins two stones. Black is helpless — he can't save his stones after White prevents the bamboo joint.

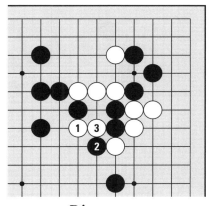

Diagram 23

Philosophical speculation: In many ways, the Alien Symbol is a structural representation of the creative conflict that is the hallmark of Go (and perhaps of life as well). Stones that are connected are strong, and stones that are cut are weak — as E.M. Forster says, *only connect*. The bamboo joint and the tiger's mouth are the twin icons of connection. You can take out an opposing force of any size with almost nothing, if you aim for the connections and the incomplete links of the chain — spoiling the bamboo joint as in the case of the Alien Symbol, or playing on the pivot as in the case of the tiger's mouth.

4. THE SNAPBACK

The **snapback**, a capturing technique involving a sacrifice, is discussed in previous volumes. Let's look at an advanced example.

Diagram 30:

If Black cuts at 1, where would you play?

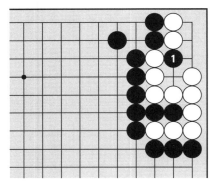

Diagram 30

Diagram 31:

White 1 looks natural, but if Black plays at 2, no matter which stone White captures, she is caught in a snapback.

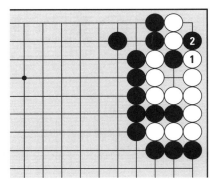

Diagram 31

Diagram 32:

In a snapback, when you capture the sacrificial throw-in you block one of your own liberties, putting yourself in atari. For example, if White takes one stone at 3, she's put her own twelve stones in atari.

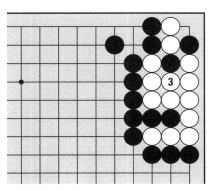

Diagram 32

Diagram 33:

So after Black 1, is White dead? Not if she is on the lookout for a snapback. White can avoid it by playing at 2.

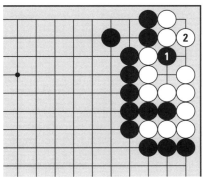

Diagram 33

5. *THE STRANGE PROPERTY OF THE 2-1 POINT*

The corner of the board has strange properties. If a stone is on the 1-1 point you can capture it with only two moves — and you can make a "tiger's mouth" with only one move on the 2-1 point. Since life and death often involves making an eye quickly, the 2-1 point is often the vital point.

Diagram 24:

How can Black kill this group?

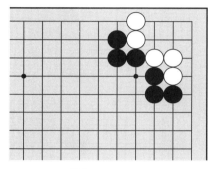

Diagram 24

Diagram 25:

Black 1, the 2-1 point, is the killing move. (The term 2-1 point could refer to either of the points immediately adjacent to the 1-1 point.)

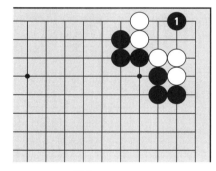

Diagram 25

Diagram 26:

If White plays at 2, Black can just block at 3. If White connects at 4 to prevent Black from catching two stones in a snapback, White dies in **gote** — that is, White's dead even after spending a move to defend.

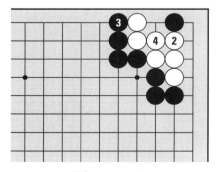

Diagram 26

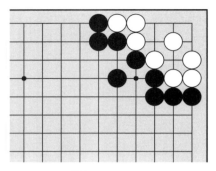

Diagram 27

Diagram 27:

Let's look at another example of the strange property of the 2-1 point. White looks safe, but Black can make a ko.

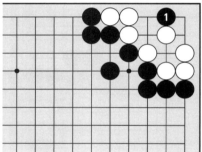

Diagram 28

Diagram 28:

The first step is Black 1 at the 2-1 point.

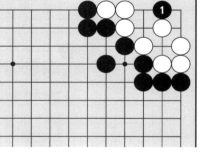

Diagram 29

Diagram 29:

White needs to connect at 2 to avoid a snapback. (Do you see it?) Black then throws in at 3, making a ko.

6. PLAYING UNDER THE STONES TO KILL

Diagram 34:

Black looks alive, because if he captures he'll have two eyes, and if White plays at A and Black captures at B, the resulting position looks like a Z bent four. However —

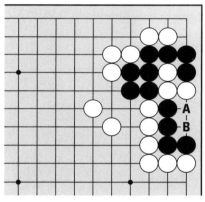

Diagram 34

Diagram 35:

If White gives up another stone at 1, and Black captures four stones at 2 —

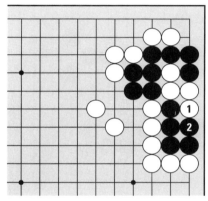

Diagram 35

Diagram 36:

White can cut at 3, putting Black's five stones in atari. Black is helpless.

Just as when you're trying to live it's important to make sure there are no cutting points in your eye space where your stones can be put in atari, it's often fruitful to check if there might be any flaws in your opponent's eye space.

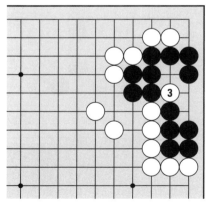

Diagram 36

7. *DEAD L*

The L bent four is alive without playing, except in one case. If a group is forced into an L with all the points of the eye space on the first line, because of the strange property of the 2-1 point, there's a ko. If the group can be forced into this shape at any time, and the stones surrounding the group are alive, the group is dead as it stands. Here's how it works:

Diagram 37:

All the points of this L bent four are on the first line. Ordinarily the L is alive, but here, Black needs another move at A or B to live. Otherwise, White can play at A, setting up a ko — if Black plays B to try to make two eyes, White can take at C.

Diagram 38:

If a group may be forced into this shape at any time, it is dead as it stands. Let's look at an example of how this can come up. To save the corner group, where should Black play?

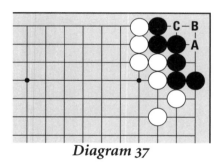

Diagram 37

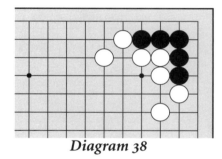

Diagram 38

Diagram 39:

If Black plays at 1, he lives.

Diagram 40:

But Black dies if he tries to enlarge his base at 1. White 2 and 4 lead to the dead L.

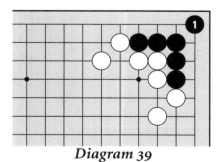

Diagram 39

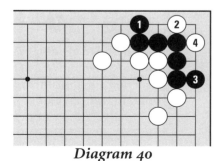

Diagram 40

Diagram 41:

Let's see why Black is dead. If White wanted to take out this group, after all the outside liberties are blocked and White connects with the marked stone —

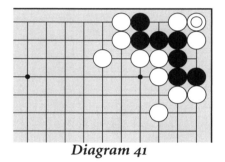

Diagram 41

Diagram 42:

White can play atari at 1. If Black takes at 2 —

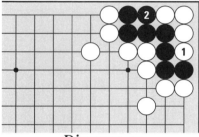

Diagram 42

Diagram 43:

This is the resulting shape after Black takes off the four stones. Black has been forced into the L bent four with all the points on the first line. Notice that White can force Black into this shape at any time — as long as White's surrounding stones are in no danger, it's up to her when to play the atari at 1 in *Diagram 42.*

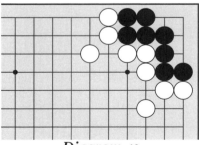

Diagram 43

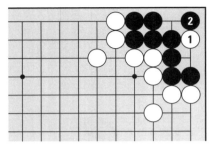

Diagram 44

Diagram 44:

Next, White plays at 1. If Black plays at 2, hoping to start a ko —

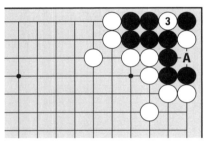

Diagram 45

Diagram 45:

White takes the ko at 3. Now Black must play a ko threat. But what if Black doesn't have any ko threats? Black's group is in atari and White can take off all the black stones at A.

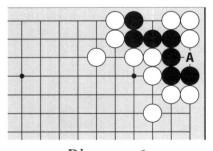

Diagram 46

Diagram 46:

This is the shape before White starts the ko. Since her surrounding stones are fine, White doesn't have to start trying to take Black off the board. It's completely up to White when to play at A and start the ko — Black doesn't have any way of living even if it's his turn. That means White can get rid of all ko threats first and then play at A. With no threats, Black will lose the ko and thus will be captured.

Most rule systems, reasoning that White can win the ko if it's up to her when to start it, treat this black group like any dead group — White can just remove it from the board at the end of the game, *without getting rid of all ko threats first*. Of course, like any other dead group, if the surrounding stones killing the group get into trouble, it may have some potential of rising from the grave — White may have to start the ko before the end of the game, in order to remove it from the board to save her own stones. And, of course, if White starts the ko by mistake, she'll just have to fight it out like any other ko.

Diagram 47:

Can White make the dead L here?

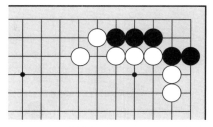

Diagram 47

Diagram 48:

If White plays the hane at 1, Black lives at 2. (If White A, Black B.)

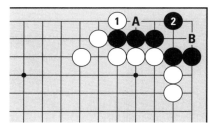

Diagram 48

Diagram 49:

White 1 on the pivot kills. If Black 2, White extends at 3. If Black 4, White 5 makes the dead L.

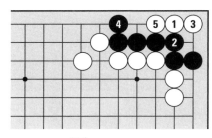

Diagram 49

Note: According to most rule systems in use today, the dead L (also known as "bent-four-in-the-corner") is just removed at the end of the game. There may be something a bit elitist about this, since it assumes it's unnecessary to play out, because the best possible moves will be played. It is also making a somewhat arbitrary ruling based on aesthetics, that it's inelegant to potentially have to play inside your own territory at the end, losing points and possibly the game, in order to remove ko threats to take off stones of otherwise undetermined status. In Ing's rule system, your opponent may insist that you play to take out dead stones at the end of the game. Since in the Ing counting system it makes no difference whether you play in your own territory or not at the end of the game, the result is the same as with other rule systems, with one exception: if there are so-called "non-removable ko threats" as can occur in dual life, then the ko fight in dead L starts for real. So, in the unlikely event you are playing by Ing rules and have a dual life and the dead L, try to play it out (or just throw a party, it's a one-in-a-million game).

CAPTURING RACES

You may remember from previous volumes that a capturing race is a fight between opposing groups, each of which needs to capture the other first in order to survive. Since capturing races are by their nature something we humans can analyze in a quantitative way, much of the material in this chapter is mathematical. So, while some of the information may be difficult, at least you know that when you've got it, you've got it. The capturing race is perhaps unique in that of all the situations that arise in Go, we can play this one perfectly. You can absorb and use the information in this chapter and then play this part of the game as well as any world champion.

1.   *BLOCK OUTSIDE LIBERTIES FIRST*

In the context of capturing races, liberties come in two flavors: inside and outside. **Inside liberties** are those that are shared by both groups. **Outside liberties** belong to only one side. If you're blocking liberties, you'll want to block those that belong to your opponent alone first, and then block the ones that you share — since when you block an inside liberty you block your own liberty as well as your opponent's.

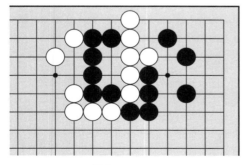

Diagram 1

Diagram 1:

It's Black's turn in this capturing race. Which liberties should he block first?

Diagram 2:

First, notice Black has three outside liberties. White also has three outside liberties. Both sides have three inside liberties, marked with an X.

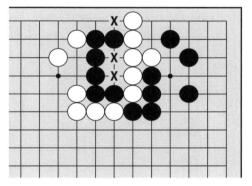

Diagram 2

Diagram 3:

Black 1 here, or on any of the inside liberties, doesn't work. If White blocks an outside liberty at 2, Black can block another liberty at 3 but gets captured first when White plays at 4.

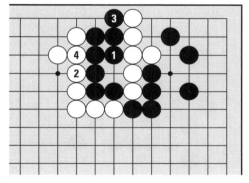

Diagram 3

Diagram 4:

Black should block one of the outside liberties with 1. Then if White 2, Black blocks another outside liberty with 3. Next —

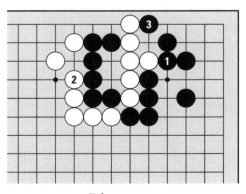

Diagram 4

Diagram 5:

White blocks at 4 and Black blocks White's last outside liberty at 5. The result in the sequence to 8, with each side playing the best moves possible, is dual life.

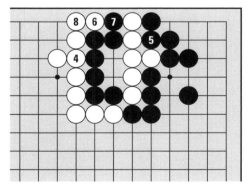

Diagram 5

2. COUNTING LIBERTIES

To find out what the result of a capturing race will be, count the liberties. If there are no inside liberties and no eyes, the winner will be the one with more liberties — or if the number of liberties is the same, the side whose turn it is to play wins. When there are inside liberties, the result will sometimes be dual life.

Diagram 6:

The first capturing race we looked at is an example of a position resulting in dual life. If both sides have the same number of outside liberties, neither side has an eye, and there are at least two inside liberties, the result is always dual life. It doesn't matter whose turn it is as long as you don't kill yourself by blocking inside liberties.

Diagram 7:

If both sides have the same number of outside liberties, both sides have an eye, and there is at least one inside liberty, the result is also dual life. Again, it doesn't matter whose turn it is as long as the inside liberty is not filled. Try to confirm this for yourself using this example.

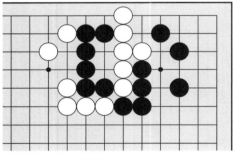

Diagram 6

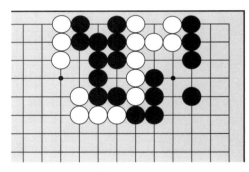

Diagram 7

You need at least two inside liberties for dual life to occur (or just one if both sides have an eye). For those who would like to be able to determine every case where dual life will occur, the "Extra for Experts" on page 112 gives the formula. Essentially, in all complex capturing races, if the result *isn't* dual life, the side with more outside liberties will win — but there are some fine points in blocking and counting liberties.

Diagram 8:

What will be the result of this capturing race? We know it can never be dual life because if there are no eyes, you need at least two inside liberties. It may appear that since Black and White each have three outside liberties, whoever's turn it is to play will win. But here, Black's outside liberty at A is a bit more than it seems.

Diagram 9:

Suppose White begins this race. White can't block Black's final outside liberty at A, because playing there would be playing into atari. A is called an **approach-move liberty.** When there are inside liberties, an approach-move liberty counts double, since it takes two moves to block it.

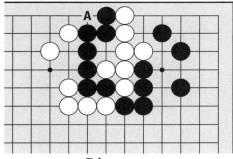

Diagram 8

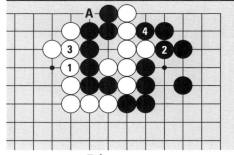

Diagram 9

Diagram 10:

How about this case? Here, there are no inside liberties, and A is an approach-move liberty. In the sequence up to 3, White puts Black into atari as usual. With no inside liberties, having one approach move liberty has no effect on the race.

Diagram 11:

But where there are no inside liberties and two approach-move liberties, this has the effect of giving you an extra liberty. Try to confirm this for yourself using this example.

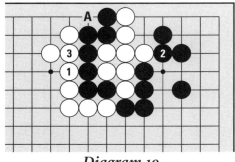

Diagram 10

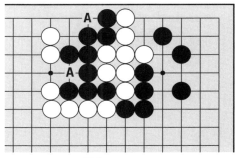

Diagram 11

3. *Eye vs. No Eye*

There's a Go proverb: "Eye vs. no eye is not a fight." What does this mean?

Diagram 12:

In this capturing race, where should Black play?

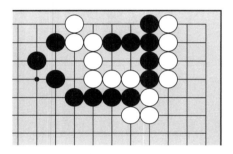

Diagram 12

Diagram 13:

Blocking a liberty at Black 1 results in dual life when White plays at 2.

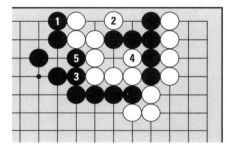

Diagram 13

Diagram 14:

Instead of blocking a liberty, making an eye at Black 1 is correct. With this move, White can be captured.

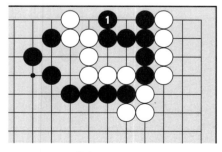

Diagram 14

Diagram 15:

Next, if White blocks a liberty with 2, Black blocks an outside liberty at 3. If White 4, Black 5. White can't play at A, so Black wins the race.

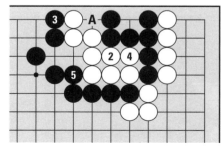

Diagram 15

Why did this happen? An eye is worth more than an ordinary outside liberty. When there's a possibility of making an eye ...

Diagram 16:

Back to the original position. White has six liberties (four outside and two inside) and Black has four (two outside and two inside). It seems as though Black can't win this race, but, as we saw, Black can make an eye.

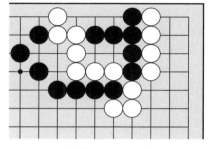

Diagram 16

Diagram 17:

When Black makes an eye, White still has six liberties, three outside and three inside. Black has four liberties, in this case three inside and one outside (an eye is an outside liberty, because it belongs to only one side). But now, because he has an eye, *he can add the number of inside liberties again to his total.* For practical counting purposes Black's eyed group has seven liberties, so Black wins this race by one liberty.

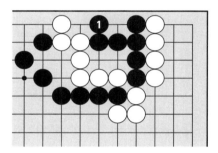

Diagram 17

Since you can't block an outside liberty that is also an eye without first blocking all the inside liberties, the effect of making an eye is to add the number of inside liberties to your total of outside liberties. Don't worry if you don't get all the hows and whys for now: the important conclusion from all this is that making, or preventing your opponent from making an eye, is a good idea in capturing races.

Special Note: To convey profound understanding, next time you're in one of these capturing races with a Japanese friend, just shrug and say *meari menashi* ("eye vs. no eye," the shrug indicating either quiet acceptance of defeat or sympathy for the opponent's bit of bad luck).

EXTRA FOR EXPERTS

From my observations, I have come up with Kim's Theorem #1 for those who may be interested in a deeper exploration of capturing races:

In a capturing race with at least two inside liberties where there are no eyes, or where there is at least one inside liberty and each side has an eye, as long as the total of one side's outside liberties plus the number of inside liberties is greater than the other side's outside liberties, the result is dual life. Put in a more symbolic way (given one of the above scenarios): $X_{out} + I > Y_{out} + 1 = $ **dual life.**

I've discovered a remarkable proof of this theorem, but there isn't enough space for it on the page.
— P. de Fermat

Diagram 1:

Here's an example. In this race, there are seven inside liberties and neither side has an eye. White has ten outside liberties; Black has six. Plugging in White as X, I as seven, and Black as Y in our formula, $10+7 > 6+1$, and with Black as X, $6+7 > 10+1$, so we know the result will be dual life. (If Xout + I = Yout +1, the result is dual life if the smaller of Xout or Yout plays first.) The formula must hold true for both cases, White as X and Black as X. But since we can see that we'll reach equality sooner with Black as X, we'll just examine that case.

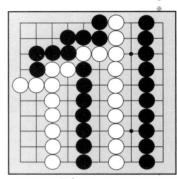

Diagram 1

Diagram 2:

If White blocks a liberty at 1, then it's $5+7 > 10$, so the result is still dual life. If White blocks another liberty with 3, then it's $4+7 > 10$, still dual life. Next, if White blocks another liberty, it will be $3 + 7$, which is *not* greater than 10 — so Black will die if he doesn't block one of White's outside liberties with 4. In order to maintain dual life, you only have to play when the left side of the formula is one greater than the right side.

Diagram 2

Converting knowledge to power: We know White wasted a move at 1 — Black could ignore it and play a useful move with 2. We know that if Black fills an inside liberty with 2, he's killing himself: $5+6 > 10$, but next when White 3 blocks an outside liberty, it'll be $4+6$, which is not greater than 10. Finally, we know that White can wait until all her outside liberties are blocked before she has to play ($0 + 7 > 6$). Imagine a fifty-move capturing race sequence where, after your opponent painfully deliberates the next play, you smile and play elsewhere.

4. *3-3, 4-5, 5-8, 6-12*

Suppose your stones have a **big eye** — that is, an eye of two points or more. How should you count the liberties of a big eye? Since opposing stones played inside an eye can be captured, playing a capturing race with a big eye is not as simple as just blocking liberties. You'll have to play moves inside the big eye, letting your stones be captured, and play inside again. Each time your stones are captured, the big eye gets smaller, until finally it is just a single point and the group is in atari. In the pairs of numbers above, the first number is the size of the big eye, and the second number is the number of ordinary outside liberties the big eye is equivalent to. For instance, a four-point eye shape is worth five ordinary outside liberties.

This only holds true if a group can't make two eyes, of course — you can't capture living groups. Some eye shapes are just dead, and some require a move on the pivot to kill them. In the latter case we have to include the killing move in the total number of equivalent ordinary outside liberties. Let's see how this works.

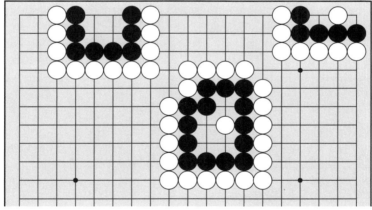

Diagram 18

Diagram 18:

The Black group in the upper right corner has a three-point eye shape with a killing stone on the pivot. This shape is equivalent to three liberties, less the killing stone for a total of two. The group in the upper left has a four-point eye shape, so according to the guide, this is equivalent to five ordinary outside liberties. The blown-out radial five eye shape in the middle has the equivalent of eight liberties, minus the killing move for a total of seven.

Diagram 19:

When Black plays on the pivot at 1, the capturing race is on. Black has six liberties. The white group has a five-point eye shape, which has the equivalent of eight liberties. Black's already played the first move at 1, so now White has seven. White will win this race.

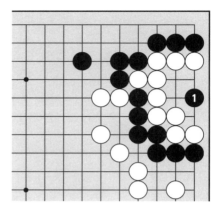

Diagram 19

Diagram 20:

White can even play elsewhere and still win. Suppose she does, and Black continues with 3. Now it's six to six in the liberty fight. If Black could play again he could capture, but it's White's turn. So White just blocks a liberty with 4.

Diagram 21:

There's no point for Black to continue now, but if he blindly continues to fill in White's eye space, White just keeps blocking liberties. Black 7 is atari, so White takes at 8. Next —

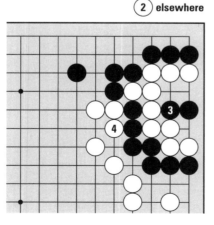

Diagram 20

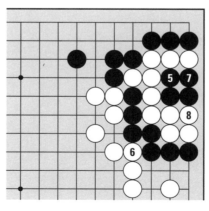

Diagram 21

Diagram 22:

Black keeps filling with 9 and 11, and White continues to block liberties. Black 13 is atari, so White takes at 14. Finally —

Diagram 23:

Black has to play at 15 to prevent White from making two eyes. Next Black could put White in **final atari,** but White gets there first with 16.

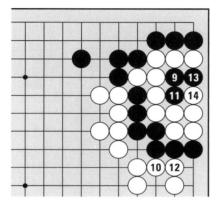

Diagram 22

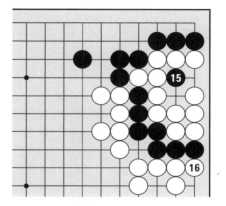

Diagram 23

The great advantage of knowing all this in advance is that if you're ahead in the race, you can avoid wasting moves. If you're behind, you shouldn't start the race — blocking a liberty makes a great ko threat later.

Also, mastering this is easier than you'd think, but it looks very impressive. Knowledge is power.

---

final atari: an atari where capture on the next move cannot be forestalled.

Note that a "move" implies a non-sente play — playing an atari your opponent responds to is not a "move", but a forced exchange. It doesn't cost you any "Go time" to make the exchange. You may notice that the number of equivalent ordinary outside liberties of a big eye is not the number of stones actually played, but the number of moves in this sense.

You may also want to consider what this suggests about the nature of Go, sente, and timing. In a wacky way, a sente play exists outside of Go time. It is *already there, yet you have the advantage of not having to commit to it until you're absolutely sure you want it and no other.* Have a look at Diagram 18 on page 65. The trick is to envision the stones in a sente exchange like White A for Black B as already existing on the board, without hurrying to pull them into physical reality — you may choose to reveal other invisibles in the space you leave.

5. BIG EYE VS. SMALL EYE

As a guideline, in capturing races with an equal number of outside liberties, the side with the larger eye shape wins. That is, if one side has an eye shape of four or more, keep in mind that's equivalent to a lot of outside liberties – 5, 8, or 12.

Diagram 24:

Black has a three-point eye shape and White has a four-point eye shape. Both sides have the same number of outside liberties, namely, zero. The inside liberties don't matter in a big eye vs. small eye fight. White will win this race.

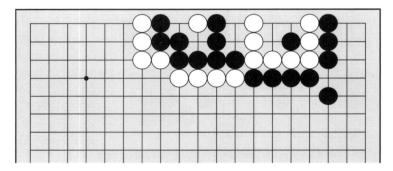

Diagram 24

Diagram 25:

Suppose Black starts playing inside White's eye shape and blocking liberties with 1, 3, and 5. White doesn't have to do anything until Black 7. This is atari, so after White captures at 8 —

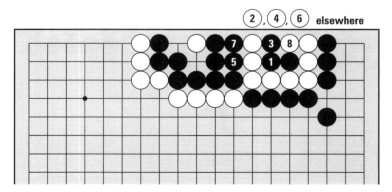

Diagram 25

Diagram 26:

Black needs to play at 9 on the pivot to prevent White from making two eyes. But White can then play atari at 10, and it's all over for Black.

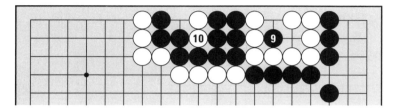

Diagram 26

Diagram 27:

It's not necessary for White to play in **Diagram 24,** but if she wants to take off the black group — which she would only have to do if her marked stones were themselves being surrounded — White can just start the race. Even if Black fills in at 2 and 4, when White captures at 5 —

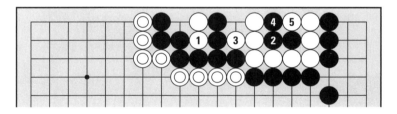

Diagram 27

Diagram 28:

Black plays on the pivot at 6 to prevent White from making two eyes, but White can just play final atari at 7.

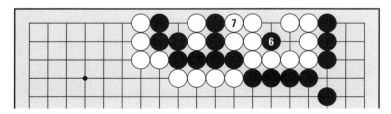

Diagram 28

6. TAKE KO LAST

Diagram 29:

In this position, both Black and White have six outside liberties. Ordinarily, if it were her turn, White would simply win the capturing race (there are no inside liberties, so there is no chance of this becoming dual life). But in this case, Black's liberty at A is a ko.

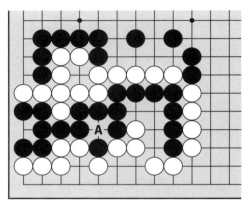

Diagram 29

Diagram 30:

If White blocks an outside liberty by taking the ko first, then in the sequence to 9, Black's group can be put in atari as usual.

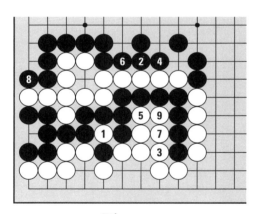

Diagram 30

Diagram 31:

But with 10, Black can take the ko, and White has to make a ko threat before taking back. If White can't find a threat, or if Black ignores her threat, Black can play atari at A and win the capturing race. (In this example, White took the ko first with 1; if White takes the ko with moves 3, 5, or 7, she has the same problem of having to find a ko threat.)

Diagram 32:

The correct sequence for blocking liberties is to take the ko last, with White 9. Black can still fight ko to win the capturing race, but there's a big difference: now Black has to play a ko threat first. It's a big disadvantage to have to make the first threat, because good ko threats are usually precious few, so this is one important and practical rule to remember.

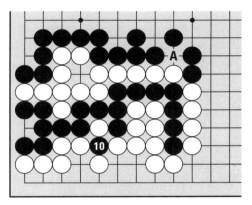

Diagram 31

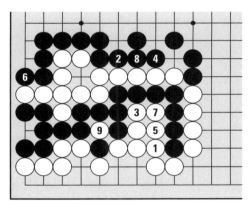

Diagram 32

7.   DON'T START IF YOU CAN'T WIN

This may seem obvious, but people often have a strange desire to play out a losing sequence to the bitter end. Count liberties and restrain yourself if you are behind. If there's a ko later, or if the your opponent's surrounding stones get into trouble, you'll be glad you did.

Diagram 33:

In the capturing race in the lower right, Black is a move behind, so Black's twelve stones are dead. But armed with logic and the right attitude, Black could make this more of an opportunity than a setback.

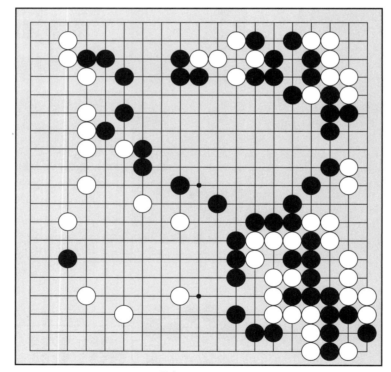

Diagram 33

First off, it's not so obvious why Black is behind, so let's take a closer look. Notice if Black plays atari at A, White has to connect at B. You don't have to consider these kinds of atari-connect exchanges in a capturing race — it doesn't cost Black a move to block at A because the atari is sente, and B isn't a White liberty since she has to connect. So White has only four outside liberties.

If you don't count A or B for White, you shouldn't count B for Black either. Black has what looks like a bent-three eye shape in the corner with a white stone on the pivot, so you might think there are two liberties here, but it's not so. If the stones are not all solidly connected, you have to make sure an atari of part of the group is not possible. Here, the marked stone is not solidly connected to the main part of the group involved in the capturing race, so you can't count the marked stone's liberty at D. Another way of looking at it is that you can't count C as a liberty, because it will eventually be sente for White to put the main part of the group in atari, so Black has to connect at C.

Either way, Black has three outside liberties. White has four, so Black is a move behind. In this case it doesn't matter that Black has an eye — adding the number of inside liberties (namely, zero) again to his total doesn't help.

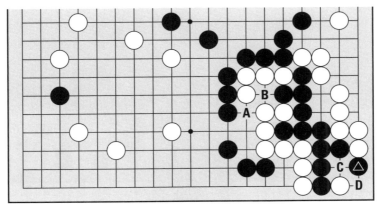

Diagram 34

It's a bit complicated to explain the reasoning, but in practice this can be fairly simple capturing race to count. First, do a bit of clean-up with the A-B exchange. Then notice it will take three moves to take the key black stones off, and four moves to take White off, so Black is a move behind.

Diagram 35:

So Black is behind by one. If he starts blocking liberties, in the sequence to 8 Black gets captured. Besides making sure that his group is dead, Black didn't accomplish anything with these moves. Instead of playing them out when you know you are behind, you should try to use these situations to your advantage.

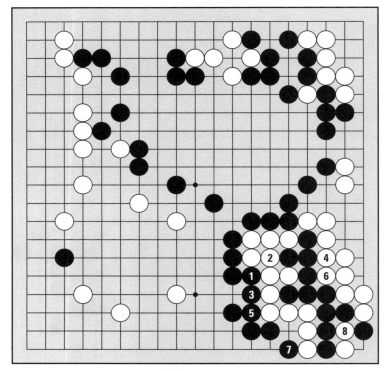

Diagram 35

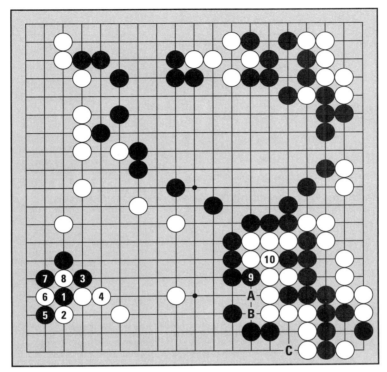

Diagram 36

Diagram 36:

Looking around the board, Black hits upon a plan. He leaves the lower right alone and tries to settle his lone stone on the lower left. He attaches at 1 and makes the tiger's mouth at 3. If White extends at 4, Black can play the hane at 5, aiming for a ko with 7 if White cuts at 6. When White takes the ko at 8, Black can play atari at 9 as a ko threat. Since Black has additional threats at A, B, and C, Black has a good chance to win the ko.

White made about thirty points from killing Black in the lower right, and has about fifty points on the left if Black's group there lives, giving her a total of about eighty points. But since Black has about eighty-five points, if he does stabilize his stones in the lower left, he has a good chance of winning the game as well as the ko.

KO FIGHTING

It's said that ko fighting makes Go twice as fun. But if you don't know the concepts too well, it can seem more like a headache. Remember, ko can be your friend.

1. DON'T BE AFRAID OF KO

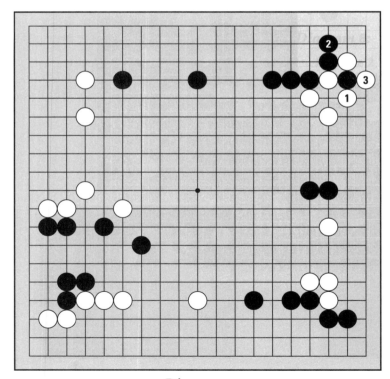

Diagram 1

If you are afraid of ko and avoid it, the result is often worse than if you fight ko and lose.

Diagram 1:

White plays atari at 1. If Black is afraid of fighting ko and just extends at 2, White gratefully captures at 3. If Black had fought and White had lost this ko, her stones in this area would have been terribly weak, and Black would have stood to make a lot of territory. As it is White now has a death star blooming in Black's area — Black's timidity has virtually won the game for White.

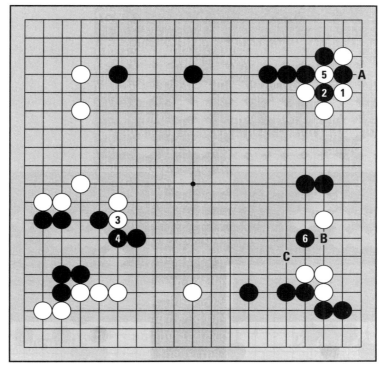

Diagram 2

Diagram 2:

Black should take the ko at 2. If White plays the ko threat at 3, Black needs to answer at 4. When White takes the ko back at 5, Black can play the ko threat at 6.

What happens if White ignores Black 6 and captures at A, winning the ko? Black can come down at B, cutting White in two, or try just polishing off the whole group at C. Since White's stones in the lower right are being severely attacked and it's likely that some stones will die, Black is satisfied with this exchange.

That's why White should answer the ko threat of Black 6.

Diagram 3:

White blocks at 7. Black takes the ko at 8, and White plays another ko threat at 9. Black 10 is a must. When White takes back the ko at 11, Black plays to seal White in at 12. White's group can be killed if she ignores this ko threat, so she answers at 13. When Black takes back the ko with 14, White doesn't have a good ko threat now, so she plays the attachment at 15. Black doesn't need to respond, but since he still has ko threats to spare on the right side, he can afford to play the hane at 16.

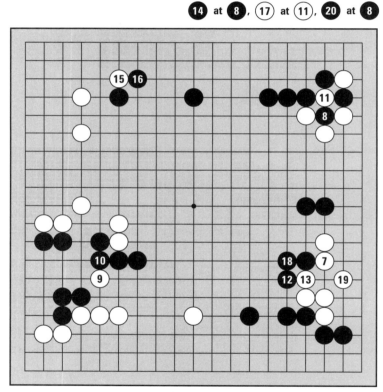

14 at **8**, **17** at **11**, **20** at **8**

Diagram 3

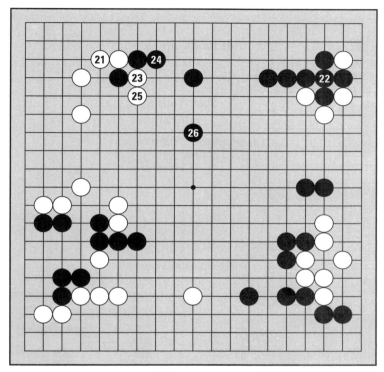

Diagram 4

Diagram 4:

Pulling back at 21 is about all White has for ko threats. This won't cause a lot of damage if Black ignores it, so Black connects the ko at 22. Black gets a big corner, and the four white stones are like eggs smashed against a cliff.

White makes some profit with 23 and 25 but a move around 26 gives Black the lead.

Black's effective ko fighting created this advantage. Even if Black doesn't have enough ko threats and loses the ko, he can still get compensation by playing twice somewhere else.

2. MEASURING ETERNITY

"Ko" is a Buddhist term for eternity. But all eternities are not created equal. You have to measure the size of the ko before you can find appropriate threats, or even know whether to fight at all.

Diagram 5:

Whoever wins this ko stands to gain a lot.

Diagram 6:

If Black wins the ko by capturing at 1, then the whole corner becomes his territory, with three weak White stones left.

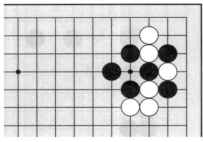

Diagram 5

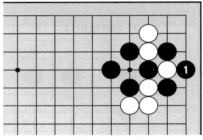

Diagram 6

Diagram 7:

If White takes the ko and wins it by capturing at 3, then she makes solid territory and truly imposing thickness.

Diagram 8:

This is the result if White wins the ko. Black's stones here are now useless. If you compare this to *Diagram 6*, you can see how big this ko is. This is called a **knock-out ko** — the game can depend on who wins it. This is one type of ko to avoid if you can't win it or get very nice compensation for losing it.

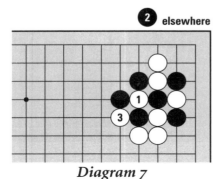

Diagram 7

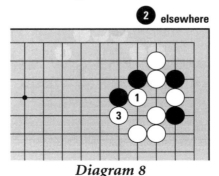

Diagram 8

Diagram 9:

Black starts a ko with 1 and 3. How big is this ko? (Notice that connecting the ko is a very bad idea for White — Black can then put eight stones in atari at A.)

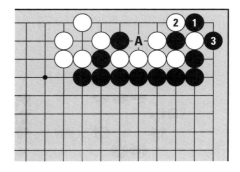

Diagram 9

Diagram 10:

If White takes the ko at 1 and wins it by capturing at 3, White will make about four additional points in the corner.

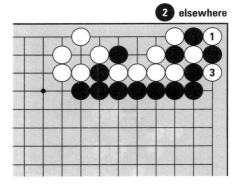

Diagram 10

Diagram 11:

What if Black has too many ko threats and White can't win? When Black takes at 1 and 3, White has to give way at 2 and 4, losing about four points in the corner. This type of ko falls into the **endgame ko** category. In contrast to the ko in the previous example, this ko is relatively small.

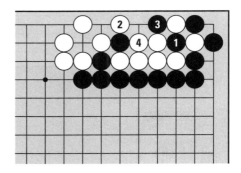

Diagram 11

3. *PICNIC KO*

A ko that is a one-sided burden is a **picnic ko,** since the side that is in no danger can just sit back and enjoy the scenery, while the other side has to fight.

Diagram 12:

When Black plays atari at 1, White has to make a ko at 2 to have any chance of living.

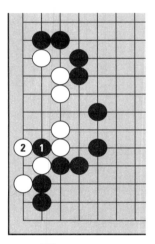

Diagram 12

Diagram 13:

After taking the ko at 3, if Black wins the ko by capturing at A, White dies. So White is under a lot of pressure to win. First she has to find a ko threat with 4 elsewhere. Black doesn't need to ignore the threat, since he doesn't need to win the ko to save himself. So he can answer the threat with 5.

④, ❺ **elsewhere**

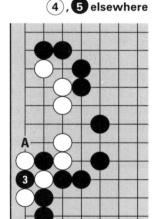

Diagram 13

Diagram 14:

White takes back the ko at 6. Next, no matter what ko threat Black plays with 7, White can hardly afford to answer. But if White ignores the threat and wins the ko by capturing at 8, there's little negative impact on Black locally; next he can take advantage of the ignored threat.

Win or lose, a picnic ko means a big return at very little cost for the side in no danger. As in life, the best things in Go are nearly free.

⑦ **elsewhere**

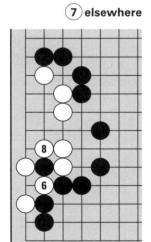

Diagram 14

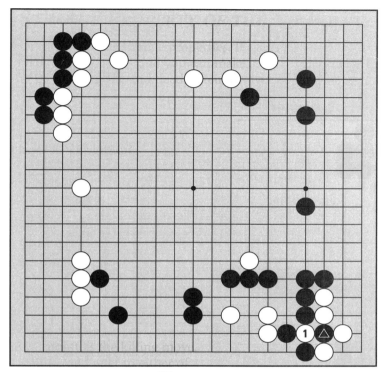

Diagram 15

Diagram 15:

White captures Black ⚫ at 1. This is a picnic ko for Black. If Black wins, all the white stones in the lower right die, and White can hardly continue the game. But if Black loses, none of his stones are in any danger. With this in mind, can you find a ko threat for Black?

Diagram 16:

Because this is a picnic ko, Black can use almost anything as a threat. Black 2, aiming at the cut, is a good one. White has to capture at 3 to live and prevent Black from locking up nearly a quarter of the board, but then Black plays atari at 4, White connects at 5, and Black catches a stone at 6. White's area on top has been completely neutralized, so Black has now pulled far ahead.

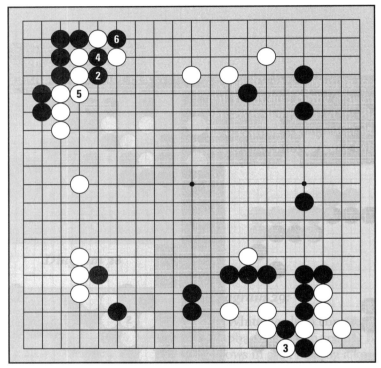

Diagram 16

4. *MULTI-STEP KO*

Diagram 17:

In this ko, Black's three stones are in atari. White can capture them and win the ko at A (or just to be weird and contrary, connect at B, although this isn't as good because Black could have some useful forcing moves later, and White is filling in a point of her own territory).

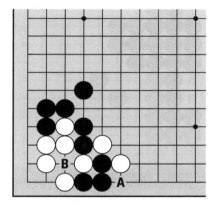

Diagram 17

Diagram 18:

After taking the ko at A, Black can win by capturing at B (or connecting).

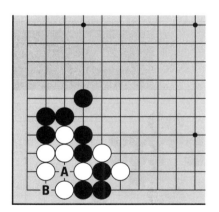

Diagram 18

As in these examples, a ko that can be won with one move after it is taken is called a one-step ko. Most ko situations you'll encounter are the one-step kind, so usually we just say "ko" instead of "one-step ko".

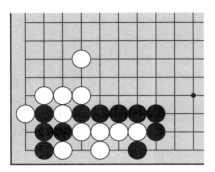

Diagram 19

Diagram 19:

This ko is different.

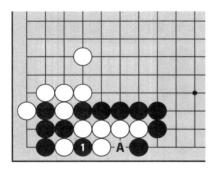

Diagram 20

Diagram 20:

After taking the ko at 1, Black can capture three stones and win the ko at A. This is a one-step ko for Black. But after capturing, White can't win the ko with just one move.

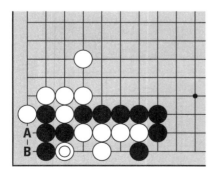

Diagram 21

Diagram 21:

After taking the ko at White ◎, White still needs to play at A and B to win the ko.

This is called a **multi-step ko**. In particular, since White needs to play two moves at A and B to win, this is a two-step ko for White.

Who has the advantage in a multi-step ko? The side that can win with one move. White still has to play at A even to make this a one-step ko, so Black can just leave it.

Don't rush to fight a multi-step ko. If you have to ignore several threats to win, the ko usually isn't big enough compensation. In the meantime the side who can win in one move is happy to answer your ko threats. This is very bad news for two reasons: good ko threats are valuable and shouldn't be used up fighting a ko you will probably lose anyway, and bad ko threats, or moves you would never play except as ko threats, can cost you points or put you at a local disadvantage.

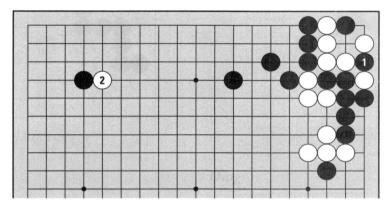

Diagram 22

Diagram 22:

In the upper right corner, Black captures a stone in ko at 1. This is a three-step ko for White. When White plays the ko threat at 2, should Black end the ko by capturing? Or should Black respond to the threat?

Diagram 23:

If Black ends the ko at 3, it's one less thing for Black to worry about, but Black should have waited. Black's upper left corner is seriously damaged by White's hane at 4. Black didn't need to hurry to win this ko.

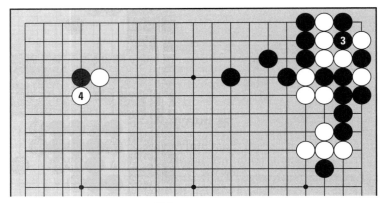

Diagram 23

Diagram 24:

Black should answer White 1. When White takes the ko with 3, Black can put heavy pressure on White's lone stone with 4. Since White still needs to play at A and B to make it a one-step ko, Black can make profit in other places and play the ko with ease. This is a hard ko for White to win.

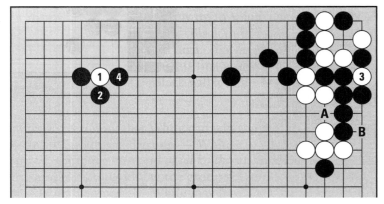

Diagram 24

EXTRA FOR EXPERTS

Diagram 1:

In this complicated position, Black can live by capturing at A, or White can capture a stone by playing at B to start a ko.

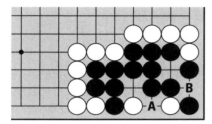

Diagram 1

Diagram 2:

If White starts the ko with 1, Black shouldn't connect at A, because then White could make a simple ko for the life of the black group by connecting at B.

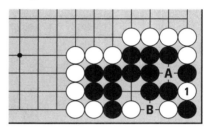

Diagram 2

Diagram 3:

It's better for Black to play a ko threat. If White ignores it and captures at 3, it's still ko. Black can play another ko threat at 4, and White has to ignore it to connect at Black ⬠ with 5 to win.

2, **4** elsewhere   **5** at ⬠

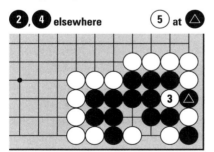

Diagram 3

Diagram 4:

On the other hand, if White answers the second threat with 5 and Black takes back the ko at 6, Black must ignore two white ko threats at 7 and 9 to win the ko by capturing with 8 and 10.

5, **7**, and **9** elsewhere

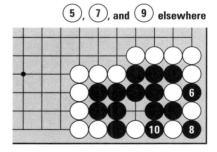

Diagram 4

This is an example of a two-step ko for both sides. White has to win two kos to kill Black's group. If Black loses the first ko, he'll have to win two kos to secure life.

5. DOUBLE KO

Diagram 25:

In the corner. the marked stones can each be captured in ko. Notice that connecting is not an option for Black.

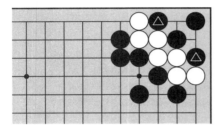

Diagram 25

Diagram 27:

If Black plays a ko threat and White answers, Black can take back the ko at 5, but then White can take the other stone in ko at 6.

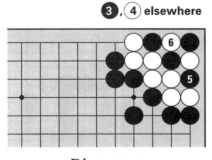

Diagram 27

Diagram 26:

If Black plays atari on the white group at 1, White takes at 2. (White can take whichever ko she feels like, since they are equivalent.)

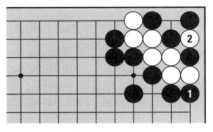

Diagram 26

Diagram 28:

This is the resulting position. If Black plays another ko threat and takes back the ko at A, White can just take back the ko at B. Next if Black plays another threat, not realizing that eventually he's going to run out of them, White just answers. Black can retake a stone by playing B, but then White can retake the stone at A.

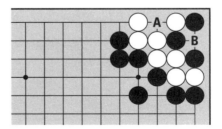

Diagram 28

This is called **double ko**. Not only can White not be killed, but she can answer any ko threat. A double ko is not a "fighting" ko — White is just alive.

Double kos are pretty rare. Here's one famous example of a double ko that results from the so-called "large avalanche" standard sequence. Although you can't kill a group that's alive in double ko, you can use the double ko as a very handy repeating source of threats for *another* ko on the board.

Diagram 29:

White can set up a double ko with 1 and 3. Black is alive, and White's corner stones are dead. But if a ko starts elsewhere on the board, White can use capturing at A, forcing B, then capturing at 1, forcing 4, as an endless supply of ko threats.

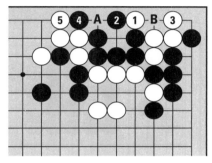

Diagram 29

Diagram 30:

Black can connect at 1, play 3 and 5, and capture White. But since Black doesn't want to spend several valuable moves capturing, this double ko might stay as an endless source of ko threats for White until the end.

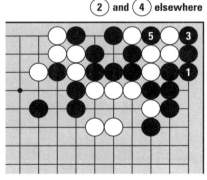

Diagram 30

There are other, frightmarishly complicated kos — triples and quadruples, sometimes involving the capture of more than one stone at a time. These are exceedingly rare. In my Go career, I have never been in one of these kos, nor have I even seen one in actual play. The study of "hyperkos" is really only necessary for the Go theorist.

6.   *How To Use Ko Threats*

The most important thing in ko fighting is knowing how to use ko threats. The standard for ko threats is simple: if your opponent does not respond, you should be able to wreak some destruction.

Diagram 31:

Black takes the ko at 1. Where is a good ko threat for White?

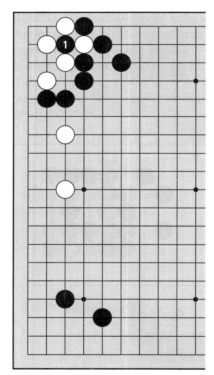

Diagram 31

Diagram 32:

What about the side extension at White 2? Since this move is not threatening, Black will win the ko by capturing at 3. White 2 is not a good ko threat.

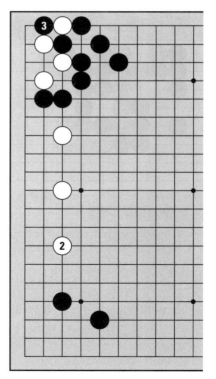

Diagram 32

Diagram 33:

If White is looking for a ko threat, the attachment at 2 isn't bad. If Black ends the ko at 3, White can play the hane at 4 and harass the black group. When Black extends at 5, White extends at 6, building the left side while keeping the pressure on. White has been nicely compensated for losing the ko.

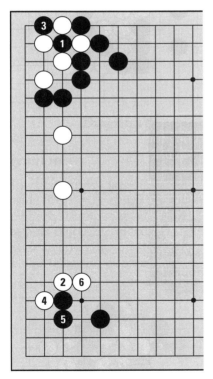

Diagram 33

Diagram 34:

Since this is a compelling ko threat, Black should respond. White can then take back the ko at 3, and the fight continues.

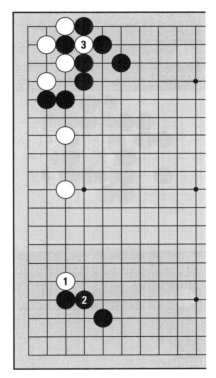

Diagram 34

One thing to be cautious about: be careful not to use ko threats that cost too much if your opponent answers. A good test is to ask yourself — would you ever play this move if you weren't fighting ko?

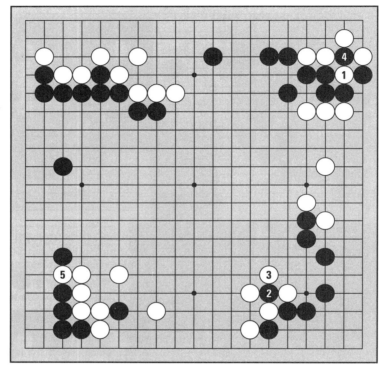

Diagram 35

Diagram 35:

In the upper right, White takes the ko at 1. If Black wins this ko, White's group dies, and Black makes about thirty points, so Black probably wants to win this ko pretty badly. What if Black plays the ko threat at 2? When White makes an important capture at 3, Black loses a lot. Black takes back the ko at 4, and White plays the ko threat at 5. Next—

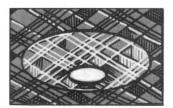

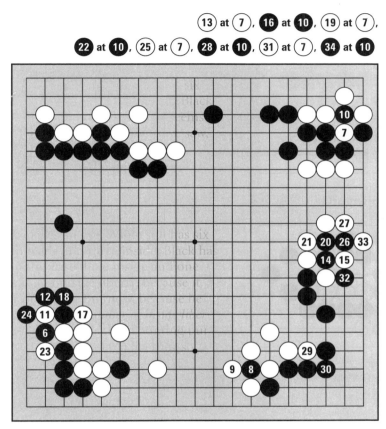

Diagram 36

Diagram 36:

Black answers at 6, and White takes back the ko at 7. Black plays 8 as a ko threat, again, a big loss. Black takes back the ko at 10, and White plays a ko threat at 11. This move is a little bit of a loss for White, but not as big as Black's expensive ko threats.

Next, Black cuts at 14 and gives white three stones as ko threats at 20, 26, and 32. Black takes back the ko at 34. White has run out of threats.

Diagram 37:

The ko ends with Black capturing at 36. Is this result a success for Black? Actually, it's a loss. The captures at A and B and the donation on the right side are worth more than the ko. Next White plays 37 and 39 in sente and then at 41. White is in no way dissatisfied. Black, in trying to win a ko worth about thirty points, lost more than he gained.

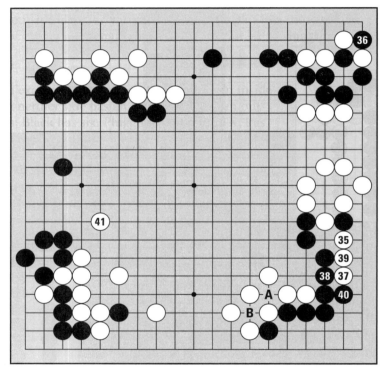

Diagram 37

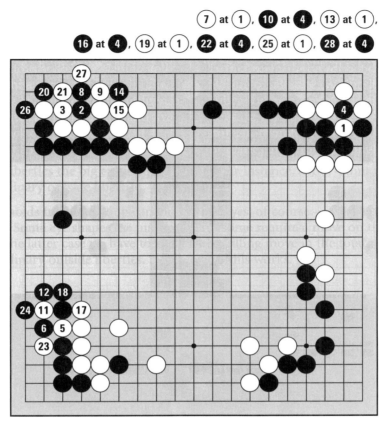

Diagram 38

Diagram 38:

When White takes the ko at 1, Black should look for a ko threat that doesn't cost too much, like cutting at 2. Since this is already White's territory, this isn't much of a loss. Black can also extend at 8 as a ko threat. Black 14 isn't any loss, and Black 20 and 26 are good endgame moves as well as ko threats.

When you have several ko threats, which order should you play them in?

Play the smallest threat you can get away with first. Why? You don't want to waste your biggest ko threats if a smaller one does the job. As an additional bonus, if your opponent answers the smaller threat, not anticipating the bigger threat coming up, you may get a lot more compensation if your opponent has to ignore the bigger threat and win the ko.

TEST YOURSELF

Here are twenty-eight questions covering the material in this book. Try to solve each problem before turning the page.

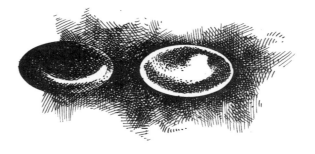

SCORING

above 20: Excellent

15-20: Good

10-15: Average

below 10: Review this book before moving to Volume V

Question 1:

Is it better for White to reduce at B, or invade at A?

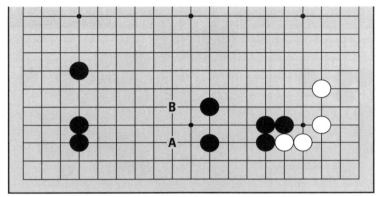

Question 1

Question 2:

Is it better for White to reduce at B, or to invade at A?

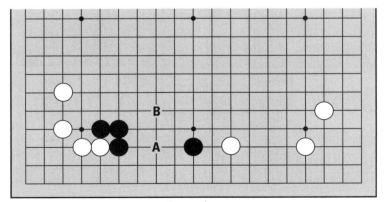

Question 2

Answer 1:

The reduction at 1 is better. When Black is thick like this and White has no backup, an invasion at A stands a good chance of getting killed. Black can cap at 1, and White will have to struggle to make two eyes. (pages 5-6)

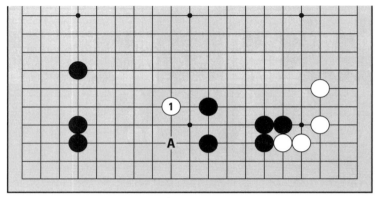

Answer 1

Answer 2:

Here, it's a shame to just reduce at B, allowing Black to link his stones at 1. The invasion at 1 takes away Black's base. With the backup stone at White ◎, White has no worries about being trapped. (pages 7-8)

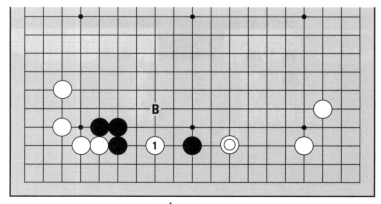

Answer 2

Question 3:

How can White attack Black's lone marked stone on the lower side?

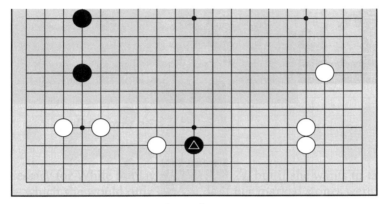

Question 3

Question 4:

How should White attack Black's three stones on the lower right side?

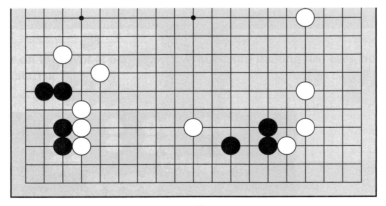

Question 4

Answer 3:

The pincer at White 1 is a good attack, preventing Black from making a base and flushing him, eyeless, out into the center. Notice White is also making some nice territory in the lower right while attacking. (pages 45-46)

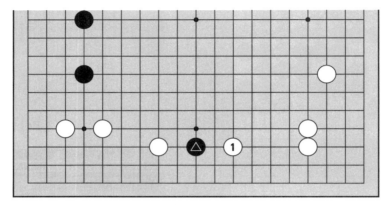

Answer 3

Answer 4:

The iron pillar at White 1 is a dual-function move, making territory in the lower left while keeping Black from sliding under at A and securing a base. (page 47)

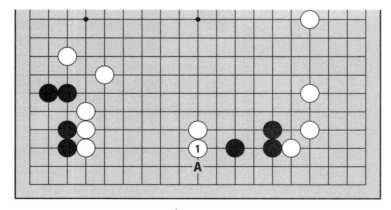

Answer 4

Question 5:

Which cut is bigger – A or B?

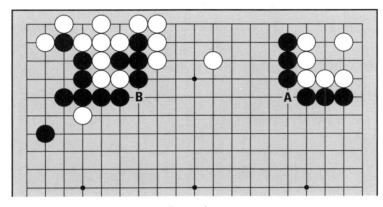

Question 5

Question 6:

Black has just surrounded White's upper right corner stones with 1. Should White make a base at A, or try to push through at B and cut?

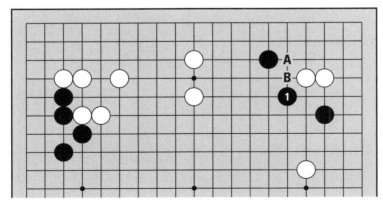

Question 6

Answer 5:

The cut at 1 is bigger. White at B would cut off Black's four stones from his main group, but these are expendables — White's upper left group is already alive. The cut at B destabilizes Black in the upper right, and sets the stage for a fierce attack. (pages 22-24)

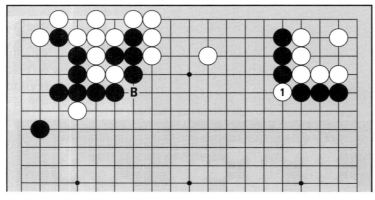

Answer 5

Answer 6:

White doesn't need to scramble for a base with A — Black is the one who should be afraid. White is very thick on the outside, so she should push through and cut in sequence to 4. Black will have trouble living with all his stones. (pages 36-39)

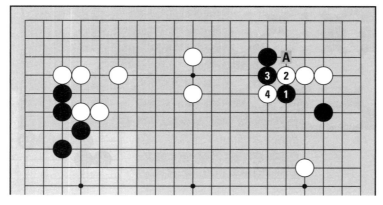

Answer 6

Question 7:

White isn't completely secure, because her base is a little too narrow. What's a good plan of attack for Black?

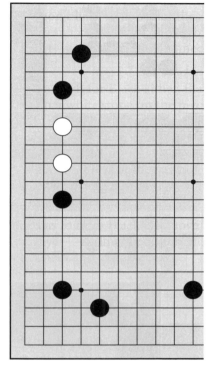

Question 7

Question 8:

White's five stones are struggling to make life. What's White's only hope?

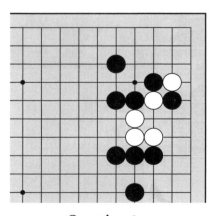

Question 8

Answer 7:

Black 1, attacking with the knight's move, is a good plan. As White jumps out, Black can follow, making a big framework in the lower left while attacking. (page 51)

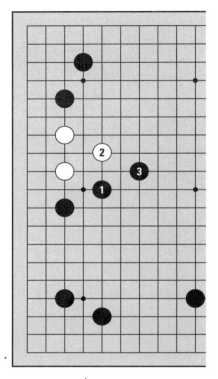

Answer 7

Answer 8:

White's only chance is to make a ko at 1. If White wins this ko, she has made two eyes. If White loses the ko, at least she will get compensation somewhere else. (pages 66-67)

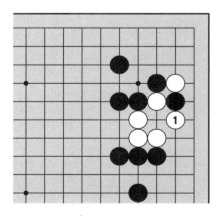

Answer 8

Question 9:

How can White make unconditional life?

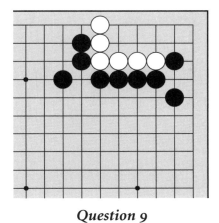

Question 9

Question 10:

Where does White play to live?

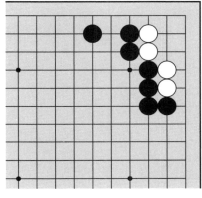

Question 10

Question 11:

Where does Black need to play to live?

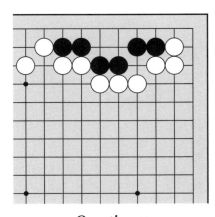

Question 11

Question 12:

How does Black make his second eye on the edge?

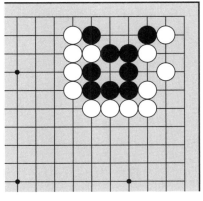

Question 12

Answer 9:

White 1 and 3 make the rectangular six eye shape, a living formation. (page 75)

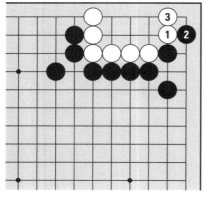

Answer 9

Answer 10:

White lives by playing at 1. (page 76)

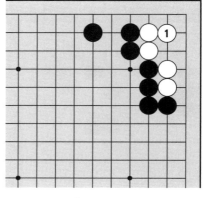

Answer 10

Answer 11:

Black 1 is the only way to make two eyes. Do you see why Black 1 at A doesn't work? (page 77)

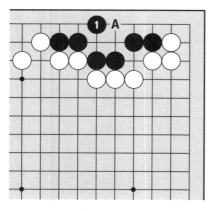

Answer 11

Answer 12:

Black 1 makes an eye on the edge with no danger of ko. Black 1 at A works the same way. (page 78)

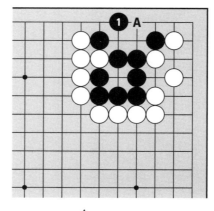

Answer 12

Question 13:

Black has one eye. How can he make the second?

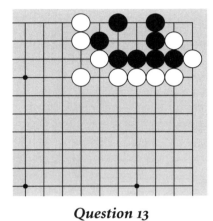

Question 13

Question 14:

Black can live here without ko. How?

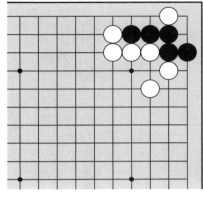

Question 14

Question 15:

How can Black prevent his stones from being captured?

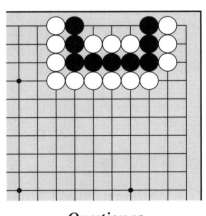

Question 15

Question 16:

What's Black's one chance of survival?

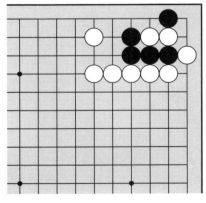

Question 16

Answer 13:

The throw-in at 1 and atari at 3 pin two white stones. (pages 79-80)

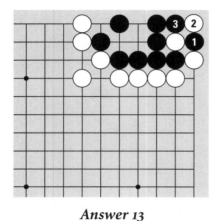

Answer 13

Answer 14:

Black can throw in at 1 and then play the atari at 3. White can't connect, so Black has his two eyes. (pages 80-82)

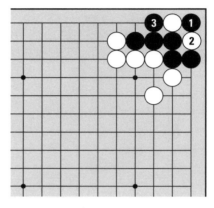

Answer 14

Answer 15:

Black 1 makes dual life. (pages 83-84)

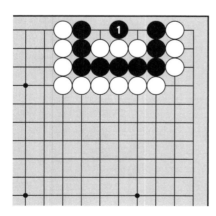

Answer 15

Answer 16:

Black 1 at the 2-1 point makes a ko for life. (page 87)

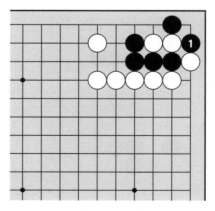

Answer 16

Question 17:

How can Black kill all of White's stones?

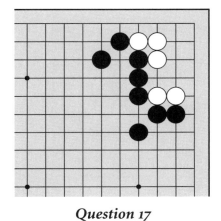

Question 17

Question 18:

How can Black kill this White group?

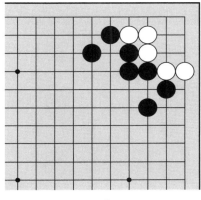

Question 18

Question 19:

Where is White's vital point?

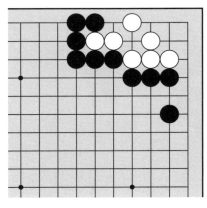

Question 19

Question 20:

How can White capture the two marked stones?

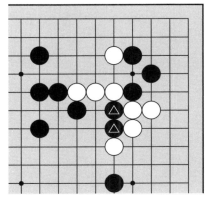

Question 20

Answer 17:

The hane at Black 1 kills. If White plays at 2, Black takes the vital point at 3. (pages 90-91)

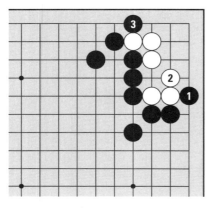

Answer 17

Answer 18:

Playing the vital point at Black 1 kills. White is helpless. (page 92)

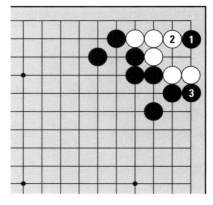

Answer 18

Answer 19:

Black 1, on the pivot, kills. (page 94)

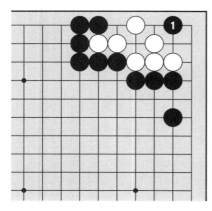

Answer 19

Answer 20:

Preventing the bamboo joint at White 1 will result in the capture of the marked stones. (pages 95-97)

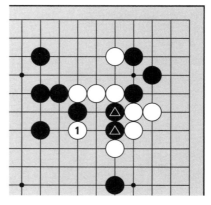

Answer 20

Question 21:

What's the status of this Black group?

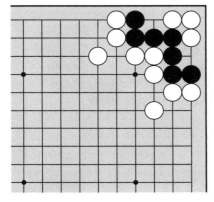

Question 21

Question 22:

What will be the result of this capturing race?

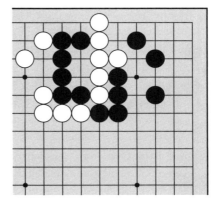

Question 22

Question 19:

Where does Black need to play to win this capturing race?

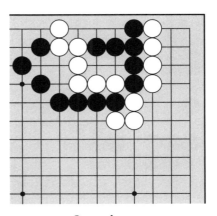

Question 23

Answer 21:

This shape is the dead L. Because White can start a ko to kill at 1 after removing all ko threats, the black group is ruled dead. (pages 102-105)

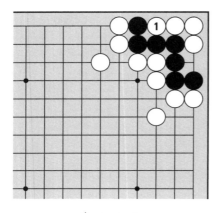

Answer 21

Answer 22:

If both sides correctly block outside liberties first, the result is dual life, regardless of whose turn it is. (pages 106-108)

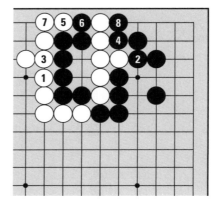

Answer 22

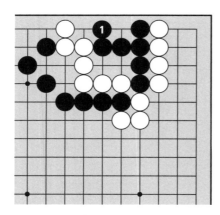

Answer 23

Answer 19:

Black wins if he makes an eye at 1. (pages 110-111)

Question 24:

What's the result of this capturing race?

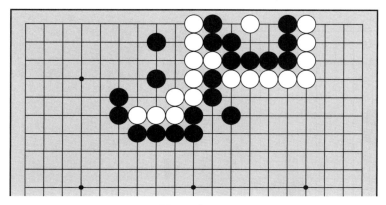

Question 24

Question 25:

Who wins this capturing race?

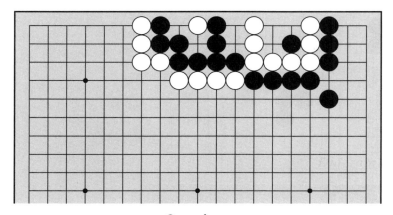

Question 25

Answer 24:

White has six liberties, and Black has a blown-out radial five eye shape, which you may remember is equivalent to seven liberties. Black is one liberty ahead, so even if White starts blocking liberties first with 1, in the sequence to 14, Black puts White in atari first. (pages 113-115)

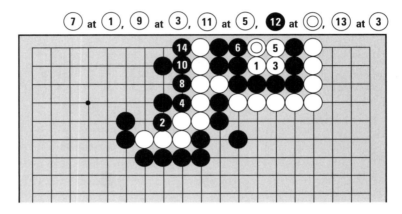

Answer 24

Answer 25:

White has the bigger eye, so White will will this race. Even if Black tries to capture with 1, 3, and 5, White can play elsewhere until Black puts her in atari at 7. After White takes at 8, Black must play 9 at 1 to prevent her from making two eyes, but then each side has two liberties left, and it's White's turn. (Pages 116-117)

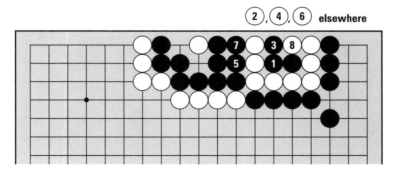

Answer 25

Question 26:

Black has just captured in the ko fight in the upper right. As a ko threat, White played 2. Should Black answer the threat at B, or win the ko by capturing four stones at A?

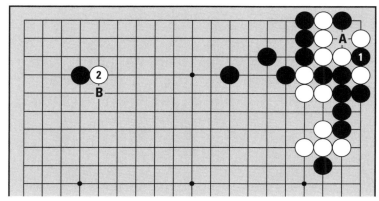

Question 26

Question 27:

What's the status of the White group?

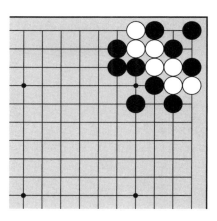

Question 27

Answer 26:

Black should answer the ko threat at 1. Black can win the ko with just one move, but White needs three more moves at A, B, and C to win this ko, even after she takes at 2. Black doesn't feel any pressure to ignore a ko threat in a multi-step ko like this. (pages 135-136)

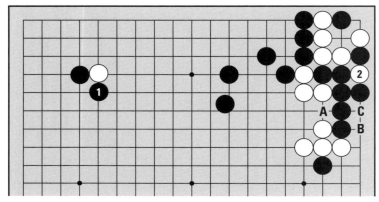

Answer 26

Answer 27:

White is alive in double ko. Black can't capture — if he puts White in atari at 1, White can capture at 2. Even if Black finds a ko threat and White answers, when Black takes back at 5, White can just take the other ko at 6. (pages 136-137)

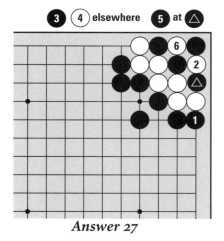

Answer 27

Question 28:

Black's just taken the ko at 1, threatening to kill White's stones in the upper left corner. Where's a good ko threat?

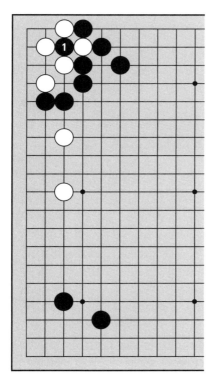

Question 28

Answer 28:

White 2 is good. If Black ignores it and wins the ko with 3, White can take away Black's corner with 4. If Black answers it's no loss for White — White 1 is a move that you might play even if you weren't fighting ko. (pages 140-141)

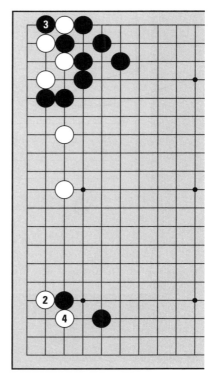

Answer 28

INDEX

Alien Symbol 95-97
bamboo joint 55, 95-97
bent three 73
bent four
        dead L 102-105
        L-shaped 73
        T-shaped 73
        Z-shaped 73
cap 6
death star 22, 55
dual life 83-84
expendables 22
extension 5
eye shape 72-74, 113-115

eye space 61-63
eye
        false 66, 91
        big 113, 116-117
        vs. no eye 110-111
flower six 74
framework 10
gote 99
haengma 64
hane 11
Ing rules 82, 105
heavy 42
high 17
invasion 2 ff.

iron pillar 6, 47

key stones 22-24

Kim's Theorem #1 112

knight's move 51

    connection 15

ko 85-87, 118-119, 124 ff.

    endgame 129

    knockout 128

    multi-step 133-137

    double 138-139

    picnic 130-132

peep 42

ko threat 140 ff.

    internal 78

    non-removable 105

liberty 21, 106 ff.

    approach-move 109

    inside 106

    outside 106

overplay 6, 8

pin 22, 79, 80, 97

pivot 40, 74, 93-94

playing under the stones 88-89, 101

power line 15

pincer 20

radial five 74

rectangular six 74-75

reduction 2 ff.

reflect 30, 55, 94

sente 37

shoulder hit 12, 14-15

slide 47

snapback 98-100

square four 74

straight three 73

straight four 73

territory line 15

thickness 14, 52-53

throw-in 79-80, 91, 98

tiger's mouth 15, 40, 77-78, 97

turning 11

2-1 point 99-100

Way of the Moving Horse, SEE HAENGMA

Note on names: Asian names in this book are given family name first. Jeong Soo-hyun 9 dan's family name is Jeong.

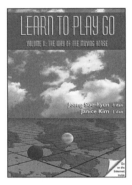